THE COMPLETE SPY

THE COMPLETE SPY

An Insider's Guide to the Latest in
High Tech Espionage & Equipment

ROBERT MCGARVEY

ELISE CAITLIN

A PERIGEE BOOK

Perigee Books
are published by
The Putnam Publishing Group
200 Madison Avenue
New York, New York 10016

Photographs on pages 146, 147, 148, 149 by Paul Haber and Ms. Fizz Productions.
All other photographs are courtesy of the suppliers of each product.
Illustrations courtesy of Ms. Fizz Productions.

Library of Congress Cataloging in Publication Data

McGarvey, Robert.
The complete spy.

1. Espionage—Equipment and supplies.
I. Caitlin, Elise. II. Title.
UB270.M385   1983   355.3′43′028   82-22338
ISBN 0-399-50738-8

First Perigee printing, 1983
Printed in the United States of America
2 3 4 5 6 7 8 9

BOOK DESIGN BY BERNARD SCHLEIFER

ACKNOWLEDGMENTS

OUR GRATITUDE GOES to the many suppliers and manufacturers who generously and freely cooperated with the making of The Complete Spy.

And special thanks to: Glenn Cowley, Ann Everds, Paul Haber, Anne Kostick, Michael Mahler, Steve White, and our attorney, Glen J. Vida.

CONTENTS

THROUGH THE LOOKING GLASS

WHO AMONG US HAS *never dreamed of being a James Bond or a Jane Bond: a contemporary dragon-slayer who roams the most seamy crevasses* and *the most elegant haunts while facing and thwarting ever-present danger? Don't believe that the Bonds, Emma Peales, and men from U.N.C.L.E. do not exist. They do—or at least their world does.*

Want to be one of them? Espionage is very much an equal opportunity employer, and spies are made, never born. Thus this "how to" book is one with a difference. Its aim is not to instruct in psychological fence mending, macrame, weight loss, or sexual pyrotechnics. What we'll do instead is equip the Bondian Walter Mitty in each of us with a passport; a key card that opens the door into the looking-glass world of espionage, counterespionage, and just plain intrigue.

Technology, make no mistake, is the essence of this world. Fifty years ago the lone agent was preeminent in this incendiary world. No longer. Not since World War II, when British scientists under the leadership of Sir William Stephenson ("Intrepid," as he was code named) developed the technology that enabled the Allies to steal Nazi secrets out of the air—literally—turning every German radio broadcast against Hitler's Reich. Nowadays spying is even more an electronic cornucopia packed with gadgets for eavesdropping, tailing, maybe even destroying foes and friends alike. As fiction it's exciting, in its ready and rough danger, but ponder this: It is not just a fairy tale. And it already is very much a part of your life.

Espionage and its tools are everywhere. The US government's intelligence community numbers, at the barest minimum, 150,000 employees. Spies for hire—ranging from private detectives of meager talents through superbly skilled agents of clandestine CIA-style firms that specialize in providing fronts for retirees from federal spy shops—add another 250,000 to the total. Foreign governments support espionage forces numbering in the millions. Private security companies, state and local police departments throughout the United States boost the total by tens of thousands more. All these men and women are engaged in espionage in one form or another. And, you can be sure, they have used their expertise on you.

Hold on, you protest: I've never even met *an espionage agent! Count on this: You are being or have been spied on: when you applied for credit or life insurance or sought new employment; or in an interview in which the interviewer covertly used a "voice stress analyzer," a lie detector of sorts that checks your veracity* without *needing to be attached to you. Friends, lovers, work rivals, enemies might at this instant be using electronic surveillance techniques to bug your car, your phone, your home. It can be done cheaply—and it is done often.*

This world is *murky, but it indisputably exists and it needn't be a mystery. Know the tools of spying and you're a giant step nearer to lifting espionage's cloak of secrecy. And that's precisely our business here. So join us on this stroll through the latest and best in spy gear—the very same devices used by the professionals of the CIA, England's MI6, Israel's Mossad, Russia's KGB, and down the list of the world's most polished professionals in this darkly glittering business.*

Professional these tools are, but they are widely and legally *available—many at affordable prices. Wander through* The Complete Spy *and you will find products that range in cost from under $10 to over $100,000.*

When it comes to prices, however, view the numbers in The Complete Spy *as approximations. While they were accurate at press time, prices of espionage tools are as volatile as the business itself. Many prices have sharply declined in recent years as a consequence of high-tech innovations (miniaturization, for instance, once was close to prohibitively expensive; now minute microphones are commonplace and cheap). In other cases inflation has taken its toll and costs have vaulted upward.*

We cannot offer rock-solid promises of reliability for the products we've featured. We have made every effort to winnow out the ineffective, but caveat emptor: *The espionage marketplace is a favorite of fast-buck operators. And we've aimed to include only established, reputable suppliers and manufacturers. Will every product work as described? If you have a question, write to the supplier directly. Addresses for all suppliers mentioned in* The Complete Spy *are listed at the back of the book, in "Meet the Makers," beginning on page 189. Ask for specification sheets; raise direct questions. In our experience, suppliers gladly provide whatever information is requested.*

Is this equipment harmful? You bet—much of it is. Whenever using espionage equipment, exercise prudence and obey all applicable laws. *Sensitive microphones—"bugs"—are legal, for example. But it is* illegal *to hide one in your neighbor's living room or your boss's desk. That's common sense. If you ever have a doubt, again, ask the supplier. Or question local law enforcement officials.*

Many readers may wonder, too, about moral and ethical questions involved in owning and using much of the equipment included in The Complete Spy. *Consider just one product: Bomb Ranger. Hook it up to your car and it will electronically detonate radio-controlled bombs well in advance of your arrival. You'll live, even if that bomb was planted by terrorists who were waiting for you. But whoever had the misfortune to be in the vicinity of that bomb will die. Is that justifiable? Moral? Hardly. Spying is and forever has been a thoroughly amoral occupation—and its tools are amoral tools. Ask that question of a philosopher and you'll get a carefully considered response. Ask it of a spy—and he'll look at you as if you're nuts.*

Enough said. Read and enjoy. Because that, not the hardened practice of international espionage, is what this book is for.

THE
COMPLETE
SPY

BUGS AND TAPS: THE WORLD OF LISTENING

IT'S A BELIEF RELUCTANTLY EMBRACED, *but think for a minute, and it becomes embarrassingly clear: No conversation can be assumed private. Tin cans with waxed strings draped from room to room, water glasses cupped to the wall, extension phones picked up, tape recorders "accidentally" left on—these are everyday occurrences in the lives of ordinary people.*

Eavesdropping is an everyday occurrence in the lives of not-so-ordinary people, also, but the tools are more sophisticated and the consequences are often graver.

Raymond Patriarca, the immensely powerful Mafia chieftain of New England, was undone by a primitive police wiretap on his telephone. So was Sam "The Plumber" DeCalvalcante, a New Jersey crime boss, destroyed by FBI bugs in his office. And spoken words are not alone in harboring seeds of destruction: Joe Bonnano (who is seen in Gay Talese's Honor Thy Father) *provided pounds of painful evidence against himself by tossing business-related notes into his trash . . . which was routinely sifted by snooping law enforcement agents.*

As fair game as the Mafia is, diplomats and espionage agents themselves are still fairer. Ask the US Embassy employees in Moscow—CIA gunslingers included—who belatedly recognized that the other side had long been using microwave transmitters to pluck heavily guarded Embassys most secret conversations out of thin air.

Are taps and bugs unbeatable? Yes . . . and no. In the next chapter we'll detail a full range of devices for foiling eavesdroppers. They work and work well. But this is a technological war. Just when a way to baffle microwaves is developed, for instance, a new eavesdropping tool will emerge, such as lasers. The conflict is guaranteed to be ongoing, but the offense—eavesdroppers—always takes the lead. Antibuggers must react to newly emerging tools. So there's a built-in advantage for eavesdroppers: They invariably record successes during the lag time between the creation of an innovative overhearing gadget and the design of a neutralizer.

Should you assume that every conversation is overheard? Although it was intended for use in a different context, the Miranda warning remains good advice: Anything you say can and will be used against you . . . whether you're in police custody or in your bedroom.

Bugs

The other side is making plans—plans to do you in. Let them—talk, that is. The more they talk, the more you know—and the better prepared you are. Because you're overhearing every word they say. Hidden microphones ("bugs") are your ears on that scene.

The other side is slipshod in its countermeasures and antibug defenses? A Subminiature Microphone, one about the size of a sugar cube, will do your eavesdropping capably. Although available in a variety of casings, including pocket-clip and pin-clasp models for ready concealment under clothing, the subminiature microphone that's your best bet in this instance is one with a Velcro mounting. Affix it under a desk, behind a chair, or on the back of a picture frame. Then run a wire between the hidden mike and a voice-activated tape recorder. Voilà! Every word in the bugged room is yours to overhear at your leisure, unbeknown to the other side.

They might stumble on a microphone that large? Move down a notch to smaller dimensions and conceal an Ultra-Miniature Microphone in the other side's lair. Half the size of a postage stamp and easily hidden, it is sensitive enough to pick up whispers from a distance of twenty feet. A 25-foot cable comes with this Ultra-Miniature Mike; again, simply make the attachment to a tape recorder with VOX (voice activation) for your convenient and inconspicuous monitoring of any goings-on.

It's supremely important that the other side not sniff out your interest in their chatter? Dispense with the telltale and all-too-often discovered wires and embrace a Wireless Microphone/Transmitter system. Just hide the miniature microphone anywhere on the enemy's turf and you'll get fast transmissions via radio frequencies to your receiver (which will interface with a tape recorder to preserve every word). One hitch: with this basic system, transmission range is a close-by 150 feet. Not far enough? Take a technological leap to Sleuth VI, which features a pocket-size receiver, a miniature microphone, and a range of 1500 feet—all in a compact package that weighs one pound. Plus Sleuth VI features six channels to allow eavesdropping reception from as many microphones.

Remote and covert eavesdropping are not the only applictions for wireless systems. Both Sleuth VI and its less sophisticated kin feature microphones that can be worn on your body to turn *you* into a transmitter, and that's an option much depended upon by police officers and espionage agents in the thick of sensitive forays into dangerous terrain. If the trouble gets too hot, your side already knows—because they've heard every word on their receiver. And they're on their way.

Prices: Subminiature Microphone—$25.
Ultra-Miniature Microphone—$250.
Wireless Microphone System—$845.
Sleuth VI—$1295.
Spare Sleuth VI Transmitters—$495.

Supplier: LEA

Deluxe Parabolic Microphone

Just what *are* those neighbors saying about you at the backyard barbecue party to which you pointedly were not invited? Or maybe you're concerned about what those suspicious-looking dark-suited men are plotting in the car that's parked a quarter-mile down the road from your home.

Wonder no more. This parabolic microphone will pick up every word you wish to hear, even if those sounds are muttered at distances up to a half-mile away. Originally developed for use by naturalists, bird-watchers, and sports telecasters, the parabolic microphone features an 18¾-inch disc screen that absorbs targeted noises and directs them into a microphone for easy pickup and hearing. Delicate chirps of songbirds, commands of a football quarterback in the huddle, and more nefarious dealings of spies and others are sponged up and transmitted directly to earphones or, if a recording is desired, to an attached tape recorder. It's an ultrasensitive, moisture-sealed mike which is ideal for outdoor applications and comes with a cutoff to block abrupt loud noises (deafening gunshots, say) and circuitry to wash away unwanted background noises.

The exact effective range varies greatly with terrain (the parabolic microphone cannot cut through trees or hills, for instance) and weather. Nor is accurate audio penetration of windows generally possible. But as a rule, if you can see someone talking, the parabolic microphone lets you listen.

Price: $399 (a stripped-down version that comes minus earphones and monitoring capabilities—it must be hooked up to a tape recorder—costs $199; tape recorder not included with either model).

Supplier: Edmund Scientific.

Toshiba Microcassette Recorder

You know you know the beans—all of them. What you don't know is which beans you're spilling when you talk in your sleep. You don't even know *if* you talk in your sleep. And in this business, what you don't know is what can be counted on to do you in.

Obviously you cannot stay up all night

every night. You've got to discover what your loose-lipped nocturnal habits are. Your life hinges on it.

Now you can sleep and still find out, easily and effectively. This Toshiba Microcassette is the answer, because it's voice activated. When you're silent, ditto for the machine. Start to blabber and it whirls away, capturing your every word. Which means there's never dead air on your tape—every word counts, and *only* words count.

Compact enough to fit in a pocket at 6 × 3 × 3¼ inches this unit can be operated automatically or manually and is powered by two conventional AA batteries. Special features include a red light that flashes when it's recording, 10 percent slower playback for ease of transcribing, and 20 percent *faster* playback for times when you're making a quick search for a specific passage. Conventional playback and fast forward, of course, are included, as are a self-adjusting microphone, tape counter, cue/review control, and automatic tape shutoff.

Price: $169.

Supplier: The Sharper Image.

The Ten-Hour Tape Recorder

You drew the short straw: It's your job to bug Buford M. Bilgepew's phone to find out what he found out in Caracas. Placing the bug is easy. The hard part is monitoring his conversations, because Bilgepew is loquacious—to an unfathomable degree. The guy just loves to talk. Asked about the weather, he'll give a blow-by-blow description to rival *Moby Dick*. You know he'll be talking to his cronies about his trip to Caracas, but mix in the chitchat about his amorous adventures, his mother, his guppies, his cigars, his bathroom habits, and his trip to the zoo, and it's a conversational Black Hole—but one with informa-

tional jewels thrown in. That's why the man simply cannot be shut off.

Face up to it: There is *no* way to avoid listening to Bilgepew's descriptions of last year's hernia operation. But at least you can do it on your own time, not his. Just hook the tape recorder to a VOX switch (a device that turns the machine on only when there's a voice to be heard), and the man's spiels will be registered on tape for your leisurely monitoring later.

Yet he still will eat through most tapes fast; you realize that. So bring out the machine for big talkers—the ten-hour long-playing tape recorder that captures a huge five hours of talk per side of tape.

It's a modified Panasonic, with the full array of Panasonic features (such as Pause Control for sure transcribing of sensitive portions of tape). Weight remains a light 2 pounds 10 ounces, but internal modifications extend the usual 120 minutes of recording to 600. So it's a machine that will not run out when taping meetings, classes, interviews, or even interminable phone conversations. And its small size (1⅞" × 5⅜" × 9⅞") means it will easily fit into a briefcase and can record from there or in the open, at your option.

Price: $95.00 (VOX switch sold separately for $24.95).

Supplier: AMC Sales.

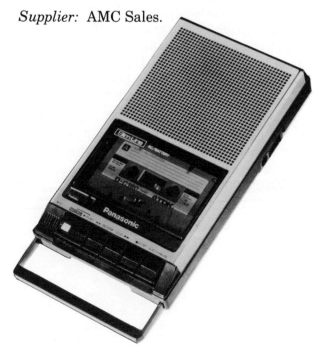

Electronic Countermeasures Receiver

You're resigned to eavesdroppers. Certainly you've implemented all the countermeasures: Exterminating crews have been through your home and office countless times, and every time they report: no bugs, no transmitters. But your secrets continue to leak out, and you're convinced an enemy bug is to blame. Besides, you have good reason to suspect the claims to foolproof efficiency of bug detectors: At the US Embassy in Moscow, transmitters hidden in a wooden plaque of the US seal (given by the USSR to a flattered American ambassador) escaped detection for six long years.

Don't fight eavesdroppers—join them: with the Electronic Countermeasures Receiver (ECR-1), a sophisticated device made for tapping into the transmissions carried by taps and bugs. ECR-1 will not deactivate them. It will not slay them. But it will let you listen in to their transmissions.

So once you've granted that your house has more bugs than a tenement has roaches, find out just what the other side is finding out about you with the ECR-1. Neither the most sophisticated nor the simplest transmitters evade its full-spectrum search for eavesdropping gear, and once it locates its quarry, ECR-1 plugs in and becomes (to put it nontechnically but thoroughly accurately) a pirate receiver. In the process it will as well indicate a bug's presence on a visual display screen, but ECR's heart is the built-in monitoring capability—a capability that enables you to bug the buggers.

Even microwaves are not immune to ECR-1. An optional attachment feeds directly into them.

Portable (27 pounds) and battery powered, ECR-1 features circuitry that will screen out innocuous commercial radio signals and false images but will effectively screen in the doings of the other side, no matter their tools. The package also includes an instructional audio cassette with sounds of actual signals and transmissions, as well as a narrative description so you can learn to decipher exactly what you are picking up.

Prices: ECR-1—$9000.
Microwave option—$4500.

Supplier: Information Security Associates.

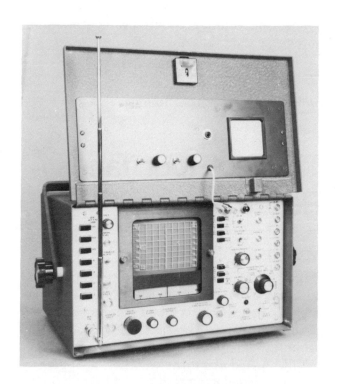

BUG EXTERMINATION

IT IS TRUE—*and do not believe anybody who insists the contrary—that if the other side wants to tap your phone or bug your home, it can. Not "will" but "can." The technology is at hand. The tools are plentiful, and new ones flood the market daily. The ability to eavesdrop is ensured. Even so, eavesdroppers make mistakes, employ inferior technology, grow careless.*

A classic case in point involved comedian and "Laugh-In" creator Dan Rowan, the CIA, the Mafia, and the Las Vegas police. It was in the 1960s, and the Mafia, it turned out, was deep in bed with the CIA in clandestine plots to kill Cuba's Fidel Castro. So deep, so cozy was that relationship that when Mob boss Sam "Momo" Giancana suspected his mistress of having a side affair with Rowan, Momo called on the CIA for help in determining the facts. Help the CIA did, although it was assistance that rivaled the Watergate break-in in technical incompetence and the Keystone Kops in comedic value. A wireman was promptly hired by the Agency and dispatched to Las Vegas to tap Rowan's phone—a piece of cake. Except he took that too literally and, in the midst of wiring Rowan's hotel-room phone, grew hungry. He left the job half done—tools everywhere, the phone in pieces—and exited for a snack. In the meantime, a maid entered Rowan's room—and immediately called the police, who pinched the wireman on his return.

Absurd? Certainly. But true. Count on the other side to try to eavesdrop—but count on them, too, to bungle the job much of the time. You can make the bungling all the more probable by equipping your team with countermeasures: state-of-the-art gadgetry for sniffing out microphones ("bugs," in the trade), telephone intersections ("taps"), and the rest of spydom's blackest tricks for overhearing your spoken words.

Phone Guard

Your telephone is tapped, and it's time to put in a call to your case officer—or maybe it's your illicit lover or your bookmaker you want a few private words with. No, you say; that's not your problem. All your calls are strictly aboveboard, but you nonetheless resent it when a housemate butts in on an extension or that prying neighbor sneaks into your party-line calls or, as is increasingly common, there's an exasperating crossing of wires at the telephone company's switching center and a stranger is given carte blanche to overhear your calls merely by lifting his receiver and listening in. Whatever the ailment, you are rankled, and what you crave is certain telephone privacy.

Fret no more. Privacy is yours with the Phone Guard, an uncomplicated device that plugs directly into your phone line and is immediately on the job protecting the security and integrity of your calls. Taps, picked-up extensions, and overlapping wires are regular fare for the Phone Guard.

Whenever there's unauthorized listening in on your calls, this gadget silently flashes its warning light to alert you. It works for outgoing and incoming calls alike, does not interfere with normal operation of your telephones, and, best of all, with the Phone Guard on your side, you are assured that your telephone is—in the jargon of spies—"clean" and uncontaminated by intruders.

Price: $49.

Supplier: Cose Technology Corp.

Telephone Voice Scramblers

Don't fear eavesdroppers. Drive them daffy instead, with a scrambler unit that's designed to turn your every spoken word into unintelligible gibberish. Go ahead, speak normally into your scrambler. But do so with the assurance that only a mated unit, on the other end of the line, can convert your words into normal, understandable speech once again.

For first-level security—high enough to thwart all but committed professional eavesdroppers—there's the PPS-225. Fully portable (just 4 pounds), the PPS-225 easily connects to any phone, and no technical knowledge is required. Simply flick a switch, turn the control knob to any of the twenty-five available codes, and start speaking. PPS-225 automatically interchanges high and low vocal tones and, harmless as that sounds on paper, when it's done PPS-225's way, the upshot is nonsensical babble for any listener who lacks his own PPS-225. Have a mate, however, and the translation is as automatic as the encoding—so conversations between counterpart units can proceed in a thoroughly normal fashion.

PPS-225 is transistorized, too, so it's on the job fast. And, for heightened portability, it's battery operated.

Yours is a higher-level security need? Step up to the SCS-370. It looks like a suitcase and the weight is only 37 pounds—but within the fiberglass carrying case is scrambling equipment so advanced as to keep your communications incomprehensible even to an expert eavesdropper.

Put simply, SCS-370 delivers assured telephone privacy three ways: automatic and pseudorandom selection from millions of security codes; a coded splitter to fragment the speech spectrum into five bands of sounds and tones; and a precision timer to change the transmission code twice per second. The upshot of all that technological black magic is voice security—security that's all the more impenetrable since there are effectively 6,600,000 codes packed into SCS-370. And not even the most persistent, obsessive decipherer will wade through the topsy-turvy mess that your messages appear to be when SCS-370 is at work.

Operation of SCS-370 is simple, however. No wires and no connections are necessary. Just insert any conventional telephone receiver into the scrambler unit and you're ready to go, either scrambled or straight—just press a button to choose your mode.

And you need not rely on telephones. Built-in circuitry allows you to use SCS-370 to transmit through a variety of communications modes: AM, FM, and satellites included. In every case, however, and no matter how you choose to send your messages, only a counterpart receiver can make sense out of SCS-370's nonsense.

The SCS-370 is powered by conventional AC current or battery (automobile batteries included).

Prices: PPS-225—$449.
SCS-370—$7500.

(NOTE: To use a scrambler in communications, *two* units are required, but quoted prices are for one unit.)

Supplier: Ted L. Gunderson & Associates.

PORTABLE TELEPHONE SCRAMBLER PPS-225

Voiceless Telephone SL 50b

Your communications from Madrid are so sensitive you will be executed immediately if anyone gets wind of them . . . and fired unceremoniously if you don't report them instantly. Yet the other side is everywhere, and you don't dare rely on Spain's notoriously leaky telephone system. That's what conventional wisdom would have, but go ahead: Take the dare. Do it because you're in a hurry but especially because you have a Voiceless Telephone in your ever-present bag of tricks.

The enigmatically named SL 50b is just as enigmatic in its communications—for those who lack the key. It's made to foil all attempts at bugging, tapping, recording, even glass-on-the-wall eavesdropping and laser gambits. Because instead of talking when you use SL 50b, you silently spell out your message on a minicomputer. Those words, in short order, are silently printed out at the other end of the line and on your unit, too, so you have a constant visual record of what

you're sending. Plus, a built-in scrambler perplexes all unauthorized decipherers with a computer-programmed code selection that's virtually unbreakable.

Want to really bug buggers and baffle the other side? In a flash the SL 50b permits you to switch from voiceless communication to speech and back again, so there's no tracking your jumbled messages. And with multiterminal hookup capability, you can also arrange confidential conference calls to as many other SL 50b's as you'd like.

Stylishly encased in an ordinary-appearing briefcase, SL 50b adapts to any phone in the world, including pay phones, and can be carried anywhere the need for silent, truly private conversations may arise.

Price: $10,000.00

Supplier: CCS.

Hidden Wire Locator

When a miniature microphone costs $25 and ultra-miniature ones can be had for not much more, no office or conference room or even home can be ruled out as a target of buggers. Eavesdropping can happen anywhere, and it might be the work of the other side . . . business competitors . . . prying neighbors . . . a jilted lover. Nobody can be flatly eliminated, and the wide availability of bugging technology makes the threat all the more pervasive. Rampant paranoia? One in every fifteen inspected sites will contain a listening device, say sweeps and security experts. Is yours the one?

Find out with the Hidden Wire Locator. Simple to operate, HWL not only pinpoints concealed wires, but also traces them their entire length—back, that is, to the bugger's base. That's because HWL produces a signal tone, which the built-in receiver then tracks throughout a suspect wiring system. Just connect the transmitter clips to the wire to be traced, and if leaks or taps are present, you'll know fast as HWL indicates unexpected "intersections," uncharted cul-de-sacs, and unwanted shortcuts.

Portable (5 pounds) and battery operated, the Hidden Wire Locator can be used on television, intercom, public address, and doorbell systems as well as telephone cables. Plus it will accurately tell the depth of buried cables without exploratory digging.

So much for *wired* bugs—which still leaves the threat of state-of-the-art eavesdropping techniques like lasers and microwaves. The Acoustic Noise Generator is made to foil them. Advanced as those methods may be, ANG knows their flaw: Both require a stable surface as a springboard for intercepting conversations—a window, for example. Just point ANG at a critical and sensitive surface and it's instantly saturated with broad-band, unfilterable vibrations and noises—noises that are crafted to intermix with human voice sounds to produce an indecipherable cacophony. Because they're vibratory, not auditory, these acoustic noises will utterly disrupt eavesdroppers without interfering with the normal conduct of your conversations.

Don't stop with windows, however. Do the same for walls by hooking up an optional transducer to ANG. It will immediately saturate walls, ceilings, air ducts, plumbing—whatever areas you designate—with the same acoustic noise vibrations. For maximum coverage of an area, as many as six transducers may be connected to a single ANG unit.

And we haven't forgotten the phone. Add a Telephone Induction Unit, and the flood of vibrations will wash over it, too.

Prices: Hidden Wire Locator—$369.
Acoustic Noise Generator—$890.
Transducer (each covers up to 6 square feet)—$75.
Telephone Induction Unit—$59.

Supplier: Ted L. Gunderson & Associates.

The Neutralizer

It's a telephone tap detector with a difference. When the conversation is secret, time is of the essence, and the stakes are so high you

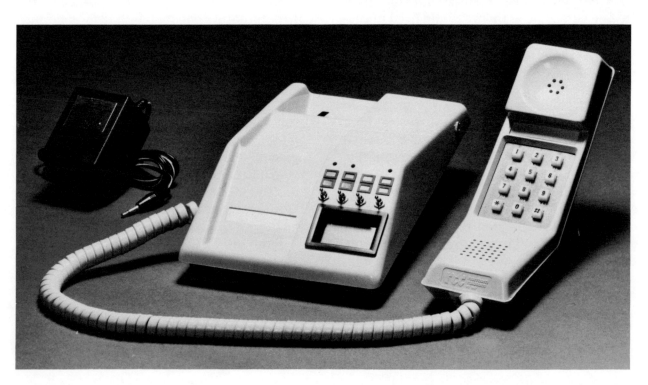

can afford to take nothing for granted—that difference can save your scalp. The Neutralizer was not so named for nothing.

The package is small—not much larger than a conventional telephone. It works like its standard kin too: Just plug Neutralizer into a wall jack and you're ready for business. In the first phase of Neutralizer's capabilities, it swiftly, ruthlessly detects wiretaps, tape-recorder activators, switching circuits, telephone transmitters, and the rest of that spooky gear. Built-in digital readouts also keep you fully informed about any threats posed by that espionage gadgetry.

But those threats are minimal and brief. In the second phase of Neutralizer's range of talents, it instantly *deactivates* any eavesdropping devices on the line. Exclusive, advanced microtechnological circuitry accomplishes this white magic—and poof! The other side is "neutralized," and your talk now can proceed as freely as you want.

Price: $1,989.

Supplier: Ted L. Gunderson & Associates.

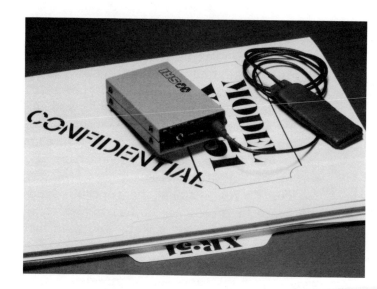

Pocket Sentry V

"You know where to meet me. Be there," the voice growls, and the phone abruptly clicks dead.

You're gleeful. You've fought for months for a meeting with the top spy from the other side. His secrets are priceless, and now he is ready to share them.

But your secrets are priceless, too. And he will want a *quid* for his *quo.* Your aim is to make certain the *quid* you ante up is never worth as much as his *quo.* But that is where the espionage game becomes a fuzzy, enigmatic jigsaw puzzle. Who's to say how much a secret is worth? In the field, you decide. At HQ, committees rule—and overrule.

You cannot permit tampering from above. Not at this critical stage. So you must keep

these dealings a secret. From his side and from your own. You cannot risk a bug, be it theirs or yours. And you cannot trust—you can never trust—that this meeting has not been and will not be discovered.

That's why you take a tiny but still major precaution: You go equipped with Pocket Sentry, a miniature but fully reliable way to sniff out all bugs and transmitters.

Only 2.8 × 2.1 × 0.8 inches, Pocket Sentry weighs a scant 5.5 ounces and is designed for concealment in a pocket. Yet it features full-service performance along with solid-state circuitry and a noiseless vibratory signal whenever a transmitter is located, as well as an antenna for a wider monitoring field.

Price: $550.

Supplier: Ted L. Gunderson & Associates.

Tape Recorder Detector

The reporter smiles. He conspicuously clicks off his hand-held tape recorder. "Now tell me," he says, "exactly who murdered John

Kennedy? Don't worry. Everything you tell me is background only. Strictly off the record. My tape recorder is off."

Fall for that and you will fall hard. You're versed in the mores of newshounds, however, so you touch your nearby TRD-800, and its silent vibrator secretly but surely sends you the warning. For confirmation, you glance at the visual display. Yep, a second tape recorder is definitely at work.

"Huh?" You dismiss the reporter—and the spare tape recorder he has hidden in a briefcase or under his jacket. "You read too many pulp novels. Out."

Saved again—by TRD-800. Small, lightweight, portable, and easily concealed, TRD-800 provides strong warning whenever it sniffs out a tape recorder. But it also doubles as a detector of radio-operated bugging devices (the most common kind) to give you a double measure of protection. Whenever either is around, TRD-800 clearly offers its dual signals—the unmistakable vibration coupled with a visual monitor that indicates if it's bugs or tape recorders that are double-dealing against you.

You need to walk around on your job but don't want to stray too far from the TRD-800's security? Plug the Dual Mode Wristwand Antenna into TRD-800, affix the inconspicuous wand to your wrist, and now you're ready for extended mobility plus fast and reliable directional examinations of your environment. (When next you're illicitly taping a rock concert, keep that feature in mind. Don't think it's a magic wand the security guard is waving in your direction. It may well be TRD-800.)

The other side is just too clever to fall for the Wristwand? No problem. On special order TRD-800 can be disguised as virtually anything . . . from a lamp to a barometer.

Fully rechargeable, TRD-800 includes a built-in battery-low indicator to alert you noiselessly to the need for a charging cycle.

Price: $1225.

Supplier: Ted L. Gunderson & Associates.

Cigar Box Combo Detector

This one is smart. His eyes ceaselessly explore your office, even though the smooth flow of words from his mouth is never interrupted. Not a man to be trusted, that's obvious. And you haven't trusted him.

Just when he seamlessly segues the conversation into matters you'd rather were left undiscussed, you inconspicuously pause. "A cigar?" you offer. And you reach within the handsome walnut cigar box and withdraw a pair of fine smokes.

Just as you thought: The concealed tape and transmitter detector is glowing a red-hot warning. But the silent alarm panel is hidden within the cigar box . . . and out of the sight of prying, deceitful foes.

Construction of the box is stylish, delicately handsome; of the combination tape recorder/transmitter detector, rugged and reliably durable. Powered by a 9-volt battery, it has sensitivity controls to weed out false alarms.

Price: $1195.

Supplier: LEA.

THE EYES HAVE IT: SURVEILLANCE, DETECTION, AND COVERT CAMERAS

CIA AND KGB FILES *are jam-packed with human casualties. Not arms, legs, and severed heads, but items every bit as personal: photographs of the victims in incriminating situations.*

The game is well known. In its most common form the bait is sex—a Soviet mozhnos *("swallow") or CIA "sister" beds a target . . . and all the while hidden cameras are clicking. If all goes according to plan, the mark, when confronted, will collapse and become a willing handmaiden of the other side. If he doesn't? Send the pictures to his government, his spouse, the media. His reputation will be destroyed, he will be neutralized. Cruel, but effective. Usually. In rare cases, the mark is jubilant when the photographs are presented. Duplicates have even been requested by a few third world leaders whose nations enjoy more permissive sexual mores.*

But the CIA and KGB, too, are often permissive. When all else fails, the guiding credo is "fake it." That's exactly what the CIA did when it hired two actors, one with a faint resemblance to the Indonesian head of state Sukarno, and filmed a grainy porno loop. It was a very odd mission, however, on two counts. For one, the film was never released. And two—perhaps this explains the first— Sukarno reputedly was a regular customer of the CIA's "cookie shop," which provided him with all the sex partners he eagerly, voraciously demanded during his US stays. How the CIA thought a bedtime flick of Sukarno—an unflappably unembarrassed sexual diner—would prove harmful to him is another Agency mystery.

Cameras, despite the occasional backfires, remain de rigueur *among spies. The CIA's training course devotes weeks to mastering the intricacies of photography, both of illicit sex and of more mundane subjects, like documents, enemy buildings, and government installations. Give a spy a glimpse of a secret document, and while he soothingly swears that what he is seeing will forever remain confidential, his concealed camera will be busy recording the pages for public distribution. Count on it: Actions and written words are no more private than spoken words.*

Covert Camera Spy System

This is one vacation your friends and co-workers back home *want* to see slides and photographs of. That's the rub: Moscow is not the District of Columbia and tourists are not encouraged to snap shots of anything that moves, or doesn't. Discouragement, in fact, is frequently so severe that cameras are stomped into tiny plastic shards by cursing guards and shutterbugs are summarily carted off to local and not hospitable jails. But you've got to get the pictures and you know it.

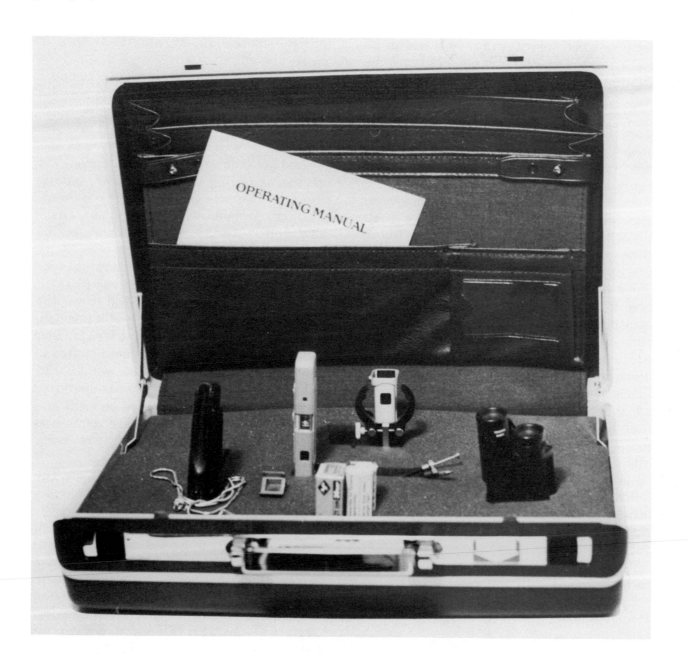

The solution is in the palm of your hand: the Covert Camera Spy System. The camera weighs a scant 3½ ounces and is smaller than a pair of glasses, yet it conveniently, easily, quietly shoots roll after roll of crisp, professional pictures. The electronic shutter does the bulk of the work. Just aim the camera, and the shutter automatically times every exposure.

A case comes with the camera, so it can be hung inconspicuously from a belt. It's tiny enough to tote in a shirt pocket. And you need not worry about scratching the lens, because when the camera is enclosed in its belt case, the shutter release locks and the viewfinder and lens are securely enveloped within their own sturdy encasement.

You say you need a clear shot of a specific man, but his importance in the Kremlin means you have no hope of getting close? No problem. When you glimpse his miniature figure exiting the black Volga limousine far down the street, clamp on the minibinocular attachment and you'll get an image eight times larger that's true and sharp. But if close-up work is your style, the Covert Camera Spy System is made for that job, too. Shoot page upon page of documents and papers from as near as 8 inches (use the attached camera chain to gauge the distance) and you'll get distortion-free reproduction, which no conventional camera will deliver under those circumstances.

Good as all that magic is, this system has a last trick—one that sounds impossible, but isn't. Remember the rising Moscow superstar in the Volga? Say you not only can't get near him, but the man's bodyguards see to it that he is always around the corner from you. A failed mission? No: Because *this system actually shoots around corners.* Just snap on the right-angle attachment, and the camera will get the picture even if your eyes don't.

A carrying case for the camera and attachment comes with the package.

Price: $3,500.

Supplier: CCS.

Wristamatic

King Hunani's fear of cameras is notorious. This monarch is convinced his soul will be snatched if just a single photograph is taken, so his precautions against that perdition are endless. One glance in his country's customs warehouse underlines the king's seriousness—the shelves are laden with heavy tourist cameras, all awaiting their turn in the royal bonfire.

But you know your assignment. You need a snapshot of the king, or HQ will have your job . . . if not your head. There was no mincing in that order. A full-face shot it must be. Or else.

And here comes Hunani's procession. The caravan is rolling down the street, coming closer and closer to you.

Hmm. Wonder what time it is? That's what you mutter, just loud enough so the crowd around you hears.

You discreetly check the time on your wristwatch and—*Mission accomplished.* Hunani's face is on celluloid, and it was the watch that did it. Well, not exactly a watch, although that is precisely what Wristamatic resembles. It's a miniature camera crafted to look like a sleek, new sports watch. But within the housing there's a fully operative camera that snaps six pictures on each cartridge (ASA 100). Negatives are round and 10 millimeter in diameter, so they're easily blown up.

Wristamatic is nearly noiseless, too. The only moving part is a patented magnetic shutter, which is unaffected by temperature. A viewfinder, fixed-focus lens, and built-in protection against double exposures complete the package.

Can't imagine you'd ever want a photograph of that porcine Hunani? Then imagine Red Square, Moscow . . . CIA HQ in Langley, Virginia . . . or MI 6 in London. Scratch all that and there's still a use for the Wrista-

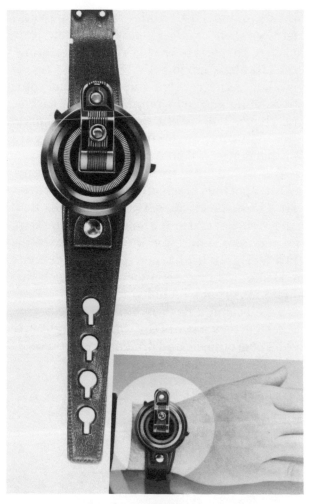

matic—its smallness and secure position on a wrist make it an ideal camera for backpacking, horseback riding, or New Year's Eve in Times Square.

Price: $39.95 (film—9 discs totaling 54 exposures—costs $5.75).

Supplier: Markline.

Tessina 35mm Camera

Take a close look at the fingernail that's perched on the Tessina camera. Study that photograph. What's odd about it? You're

right: The proportions are all wrong. Except they aren't. That's because the Tessina is the world's smallest, lightest 35 mm camera.

The claim is made without hedges. There is need for none. The Tessina is lighter than a wallet—it weighs a scant 5½ ounces—and smaller than a pack of cigarettes (it's 2½″ × 2″ × 1″). And yet it's a fully versatile and easily used camera that will yield top-quality photography any time a 35 mm camera is right for the job.

All the marvels of advanced Swiss precision and miniaturization are packed into the tiny Tessina and its 25 mm wide-angle lens. Construction is solid and virtually indestructible, and the Tessina uses conventional 35 mm film (like Kodak Tri-X). Plus there's a built-in motor wind that, at the push of a finger, will automatically take six to ten 1-by-1-inch shots.

A wide range of options and accessories is available, too. Need a noiseless camera for those extremely sensitive, perilous missions? There's a Tessina that fills the bill. There are cable releases, self-loaders, and an optional Swiss timepiece that attaches directly to the camera. Tripods, flashguns, and a choice of finishes (red, gold, and black) are also available.

So no matter how covert the assignment and how candid the photography must be, the Tessina can be equipped to do the job professionally, accurately, and discreetly.

Price: $349.50 (options raise the price to $500.00 and higher).

Supplier: Karl Heitz.

Weathermatic-A

It sounded simple enough. You're to snap a few photographs of the enemy missile site—and make like a marathoner to the nearby river. Just dive in, the briefing continued, swim to the powerboat, and you'll be ferried to safety.

Except—you snap your fingers in an ominously disconcerting realization—you've got the camera in your possession while you're swimming. It will get soaked, ruined, and so will the film. The mission will be a wash, a catastrophe.

Unless your camera is the Weathermatic-A, the world's first watertight pocket camera. Totally sealed against all weather elements (water, snow, and cold included), Weathermatic-A is made for operating under rugged conditions. Focusing and camera adjustment controls are simple, easy to use, and oversize (for convenient use while wearing gloves). Just focus and you're ready to shoot. The targeted images are crisply recorded on standard 110 film cartridges.

What if the camera tumbles out of your hands while you're swimming in that turbulent river? The bright yellow case ensures high visibility, and since it's watertight, Weathermatic-A floats, too.

You're an inveterate shutterbug and you've spotted a spectacular underwater vista? Dive down to get a better look and bring Weathermatic-A along. It will function fine and take superb pictures down to depths of 15 feet. You'll also get a wide 45-degree-angle shot (34 degrees under water) with the 26 mm lens that's included

An electronic flash is built in, and a single AA battery powers the works. Weight is a light 12$\frac{3}{16}$ ounces, and dimensions are 1$\frac{7}{8}$ × 2$\frac{13}{16}$ × 7$\frac{1}{2}$ inches.

Price: $165.

Supplier: Minolta.

Robot RSK II Camera

It may not be Big Brother, but with its exotic and austere alphabet soup name and its range of photographic functions, the Robot RSK II certainly qualifies as Little Brother.

When next you're in a police station . . . cashing a check at the market . . . visiting a bail bondsman . . . making a bet at the track . . . well, smile, because the Robot Surveillance Camera may be smiling back.

Or maybe it is you who has the Robot on the job, taking pictures of every visitor to your home or office or snapping shots of anybody who dares go near your precious Porsche.

The ever-vigilant, never-tiring Robot is crafted to handle those surveillance assignments. It's a 35mm camera that sits on a high shelf or ledge—and just waits to snap the mugs of all who enter its field of vision. Operation is fully automatic and noiseless, and the Robot will wear either a 35mm lens for fast action or a wide-angle 28mm for a broader view. Choose whichever lens you prefer; the Robot will still take 435 exposures (at speeds as fast as 2 frames per second) on a single roll of film—and those exposures make for crisp, clear pictures to cinch identification of a suspect.

And you choose how to trigger the Robot. There's a remote release and control unit; a pedal switch for unobtrusive triggering by foot; a currency drawer contact plate (for in-store uses); and releases operated by alarms and emergency devices. Custom triggers can also be designed for rarer, and more dangerous, applications.

Superb as the police-tested and approved Robot is at security functions, don't limit it to a narrow range of work. It hungers for more because it's a fully functional camera and is equally adept at snapping rapid-fire sports pictures or photographs of any fast-moving event.

The Robot isn't easily dissuaded from its work. The recessed lens sees to that—its setback position sharply reduces an intruder's chances of shattering the lens. And the unit's rugged housing locks to keep its contents within. With all but the most insistent attackers, the Robot will have the last laugh: evidence of any assault on the Robot itself will be immortalized on film. And that's powerful testimony in any court.

Price $1499 (optional control units cost $100–$200).

Supplier: Karl Heitz.

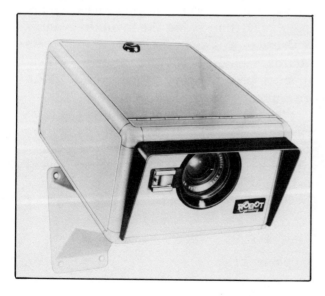

Hidden Camera System

Smile—you're on Candid Stereo Speaker? That's exactly what Model 701 appears to be—but isn't. The wood-frame cabinet is but a handsome sham. Woofers and tweeters are not inside. Instead there's a hidden camera that's activated by the ultrasonic motion detector that is also housed in Model 701. To get this wickedly concealed unit on the job, simply place it on a shelf or table and it's ready to go. Let an intruder enter the turf it over-

sees (a range adjustable from 5–30 feet), and the ultrasonic detector immediately senses the alien presence. That news is flashed to the camera, which promptly gets busy automatically snapping two frames per second (for a maximum 2000 pictures and 16 minutes total running time). And all is done silently and without alerting the unwanted guest to Model 701's dauntless surveillance. When the intruder departs, the camera stops taking pictures. But you've got a vivid record of the entry plus an indisputable photographic inventory of all that was done and taken under Model 701's electronic eyes.

Film size is 16mm, and there's a choice of a 17mm or a 25mm lens. Powered by AC current or a built-in DC battery, Model 701 is 17 inches wide by 9 inches deep by 5¾ inches high. Weight is 12½ pounds.

Price: $618 (with standard 17mm lens; add $12 for 25mm).

Supplier: C.F.I. Camera Division.

Manikin Camera

You're prowling through the enemy's lair and—strange—you could have sworn the manikin blinked at you. The anxiety of this mission is working on your nerves, you suppose. Edginess is making your eyes play tricks on you.

Nope. Guess again. There's a trick here, but it's not the work of your eyes. You're under surveillance and the manikin is doing it. Because this manikin is no dummy. Its innards include a motion detector which, when tripped, silently triggers a built-in Super-8 movie camera.

When the motion stops, so does the camera. But whenever uninvited intruders are afoot, the hidden camera records every move within its 60-degree field of vision. Every cartridge holds up to sixty hours of film, and power is provided by a battery.

Price: $2800.

Supplier: LEA.

Automatic Film Processor

The hidden miniature cameras are clicking away, and you're accumulating roll upon roll of critical, sensitive film—including those "must destroy" shots of your own extracurricular playmates. Question is, how do you get this film developed fast and *securely?*

Take it to a commercial lab and that's that for security. Everybody will see what your cameras have been watching. Do it yourself with the standard equipment, however, and it's a thoroughgoing mess, with ineradicable puddles of fixer, developer, and the rest of that chemical feast staining your floors.

But there is a way to do it yourself, fast and neatly: with a convenient P-10 Film Processor. Feed this ravenous machine up to 100 feet of film per hour, press a few buttons, and out will pop—automatically—professional-quality work. And the P-10 isn't finicky. It readily processes all types of film, including microfilm and gargantuan 70mm–wide film. And it does all this in house, for maximum security.

The P-10 is self-threading, can develop short batches without running water, and with the addition of an optional loader, will even work its magic in bright daylight, so there's no need to closet it in the darkness most developers require. The machine's size is just 36 inches long by 11 inches wide by 11 inches high. Weight is 60 pounds.

Prices: P-10—$2790.
Daylight Loader Option—$470.

Supplier: C.F.I. Camera Division.

Zenith Video Sentinel

Just back from a top-secret coup in Tierra del Fuego, you're in a festive mood, and that's why you're throwing a surprise party for the boss who dispatched you there. This surprise will be all the keener because Old Crusty Cross is convinced nobody appreciates him. He also thinks nobody can catch him unaware. But your party will be Crusty's double undoing.

With the Zenith Video Sentinel watching the door, you'll have advance warning of Crusty's approach, so you can quiet the assembled guests and even let the knocking Crusty cool his heels awhile at the locked door—all the time no doubt cursing you for screwing up again. Goad him a mite more by grilling him through the intercom, and finally waltz to the door just before he erupts. Open it, usher Crusty in, and watch his veneer crack as kisses, flowers, and presents come his way.

Handy not just for orchestrating surprise-party shenanigans, the Zenith Video Sentinel can be counted on to monitor any indoor or outdoor location. With it in place, any door can be safely answered from inside—and you'll still have a clear view of who's calling plus direct two-way voice communication with visitors for reliable, safe screening of all comers.

The system comes complete with a 12-inch black-and-white VHF/UHF TV set, intercom, video camera with a stand, 60-foot camera-TV hookup cable, 25-foot intercom-TV cable, and a button that quickly attaches to existing doorbells.

Price: $349.95 (assembled)

Supplier: Heathkit

Night Vision Goggles

You've mentally rehearsed the steps of this mission hundreds of times. Not because of this night's operation itself; that's simple work. It's the escape that's the problem. Once more you review the plan: Immediately after finishing the job, you're to hop on a motorcycle and swiftly drive down the deeply pitted and rutted dirt path. Then it's into the sewers of Paris on foot for a two-mile sprint to the Embassy . . . and up through the trapdoor into the safety of that sanctuary.

On paper it sounds relatively easy. None of it is beyond your talents. *Except* it all must be accomplished in absolute darkness. Within moments of the snatch a secret alarm will sound and guards will be hunting for you. Use the smallest light, ignite the motorcycle's beams—and that may be enough to attract this alerted and angry enemy. Just a single flash and your mission—as well as your life—could go up in flames. So darkness it must be. Yet you do not relish roaring a cycle down that pockmarked road at night without being able to see. Or running blind through Parisian sewers slick with sludge and squeaky, sharp-toothed creatures.

Don't jeopardize the mission with a light—but see clearly anyway. Use Night Vision Goggles. Developed for use by military pilots on nighttime flights, Night Vision Goggles employ an infrared principle to transform pitch blackness into sharp daylight. You'll never be left in the dark again. And since these are goggles, your hands are free for all action that the night presents.

Wear them and, dark as the evening is, Night Vision Goggles will let you see every rut in the road, every rat in the sewers. They

provide no trace of their presence. Operation is wholly passive, and surveillance will not detect them. So they're much favored by military personnel and spies as well as flight crews.

Automatic brightness control is built in, and while supplemental illumination is not required for normal operation, a small infrared light can be activated for close-up viewing of maps and like documents. A separate viewer for each eye allows for quick adjustment and focusing to keep your vision ever sharp at night . . . in dense smoke . . . in pea-soup fog.

Price: $8,000.

Supplier: Ted L. Gunderson & Associates.

Fujinon Binoculars

The easy part of this mission is the brisk but noiseless swim across the English Channel at night. The hard part happens once you hit the French coast. There, while engulfed in fog and sea mist, you must sharply train your binoculars on the inlets in search of the suspected terrorist staging dock. You know you will need powerful, reliable, but lightweight binoculars for this operation. But that is just the beginning of your demands. You also need waterproof binoculars, because soggy, clouded ones will do no good here.

Try that stunt with most binoculars and you'll wind up seeing nothing—except, that is, water streaked, blurred, and impenetrable lenses that may *never* dry out.

Fujinon binoculars provide a happier, drier ending to the story. Built to military specifications and rigorously inspected by Japan's defense ministry, these binoculars have been put to the extremes—and they have survived. One test, for instance, involved submersion in six feet of seawater for two weeks. That would destroy most binoculars; but the Fujinon remained intact. Not a drop of corrosive saltwater had penetrated the air- and water-tight rubber coating. That's the tradition that makes Fujinon a superb choice for any marine use and also for times when heavy rainfall is anticipated. Besides, the light weight (under 4 pounds) assures that Fujinon binoculars will be as comfortable and convenient as any all-purpose binoculars.

Manufactured by Japan's most experienced optical glass producer, these binoculars also feature high-quality lenses and a patented Electron Beam Coating that affords brightness without glare or flare. Power is 7-by-50 magnification, and protective rubber caps that flip up to cover the lenses are included.

A carrying case with straps is available as an option.

Price: $278.88 (carrying case—$22.77).

Supplier: Goldbergs' Marine.

Wide-Angle Minibinocular

Your assignment is at the Harvard-Yale game and—congratulations—this year it's not your job to monitor the on-field action while filling in the play-by-play for the nearly blind director of operations. This year marks a promotion.

You eye the lady in red. Her swarthy features make her unmistakable as she nonchalantly scans the game's action from her box seat on the fifty-yard line.

But the thin blond man dressed in black, your other mark, is anxiously perched in the end zone. He was supposed to accompany the lady in red, damnit.

You must cover both. That was your assignment and, hell, you don't want to go back to providing the play-by-play. Harvard-Yale, well, that's fine. But who wants to keep close tabs on the always-boring Brown game?

Out of your pocket emerges this sleek 8-by-20-power minibinocular. It's a common enough sight, binoculars at a football game. But this pair is special and is not made for sports watching alone. An expansive wide-angle field of view pops into sharp focus—you're able to target in on a 60-degree span of action (compared to the confining 50 degrees

that's typical), and that translates into a 431-foot-visible area at 1000 yards. Bingo: The lady in red and the thin blond man both leap into focus. Bravo; you're spared the Brown and even the Penn game. Well done!

So is the manufacture and design of this binocular. It's tiny—just 4 inches wide and 3 inches long. Weight is a mere 7.8 ounces. It features center focus, individual eye adjustments, and coated lenses. It comes with a handy neck band and a zippered vinyl case with a carrying strap.

And certainly it's fine for sports, nature, and plain avocational sightseeing, too.

Price: $95.

Supplier: Brookstone.

Headband Magnifier

Getting eyestrain from your tedious pasting together of that 20-page document you found shredded into noodle-size strips? The laborious effort is worth it—there is no telling what commendation this coup will win for you. But only if your eyes stay steady. It will not do to turn in gibberish to the commander.

Relax: The headband magnifier is at your service. A clever way to provide magnification while allowing both hands to proceed freely with the work, this visorlike device is

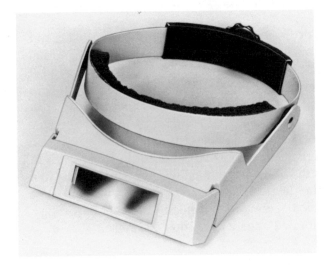

lightweight and yet enlarges miniature or detailed work one and three quarter times for clear visibility. It will work with eyeglasses and features a single-lens design (there's no annoying, distracting center post) for clear vision and reduced eyestrain. The lens is optical quality, shatter-resistant acrylic that provides a working distance of 8 to 14 inches.

The headband is plastic, with comfortable padding, and adjusts to fit any size head.

An able assistant when it comes to document reassembly, the headband magnifier is perfect for a variety of other tasks, like jewel or stamp inspection. Repairmen, tool and die makers, model builders, hobbyists, and, yes, espionage agents will all benefit from this no-hands-needed method of magnification.

Price: $14.95.

Supplier: Brookstone.

Illuminated Magnifier

It is four in the morning. For hours you've been rummaging through the trash behind Lady Droolip's manor. You begin to give up hope—maybe the tip was a prank, you scowl. But no, it can't be. The Droolip butler is owned lock, stock, and pederasty by the Agency. His—ahem—indiscretions have seen to that.

Just when you begin to conjure up the cruelest punishments for the butler, you find it—the priceless stamp with the even more priceless snippet of a confidential microdot pasted to its back, all of which the dotty Lord Droolip had angrily discarded because he thought the drawing of the loinclothed Indian was obscene.

Thank god for morality, you applaud. Then to make sure it's the authentic item, you check it out with the Illuminated Magnifier—a compact (6^7/8-inch-long) viewing tool that features $10 \times$ power plus a built-in light bulb to cast illumination in poor and dark conditions. A good choice under this circumstance, especially since the lens diameter is 1^1/8-inch and that's especially large. Plus the removable metal window has scales for making comparative measurements of tiny objects (like stamps and microdots). All powered by two standard flashlight batteries.

Price: $10.95.

Supplier: Brookstone.

Inspector's Loupe

The midnight communiqué contains photographs of the Inaugural Ball—and an urgent question scrawled in red: Who is the bearded man at the President's elbow? You stare and stare, but somehow your eyes cannot pick up enough detail to make the identification. Until you check it out with this Inspector's Loupe and blow up the face to fifteen times its true size.

Developed in a Swiss watch factory for precise quality and manufactured in Japan to hold down costs, this device is three loupes in one convenient package. Just unscrew the two sections and the large lens gives $6\times$ power; the smaller lens gives $8\times$. That choice assures versatility and makes this loupe a sure aide in inspecting gems, coins, stamps; looking for forgeries in currencies and stock certificates; and just whenever you want a closer look.

Both lenses are optical-grade polished glass, and this is one loupe that works well with eyeglasses. Total size is 1¾ inches high; maximum diameter is 1½ inches.

Price: $6.25.

Supplier: Brookstone.

Zoom Refractor

The last mission was a success; the denouement, less so. Bravo, your superiors applauded. Get underground and soon, they added. Because the flap that followed in the wake of your work was causing consternation and far worse in global diplomatic circles.

Now you're looking for that truly inaccessible hideout. And your search so far is fruitless.

That will all change when the Tasco Zoom Refractor is brought into the hunt. It's the tool to have when you're checking out remote islands far removed from any shore . . . or even the craters on the moon. Nothing eludes its searching view.

That's because when you twist the 15-pound eyepiece, it smoothly slides from 20- to 60-power magnification for a probing look at near and far fields. Freely swivel it on its 66-inch tripod to track a shooting star—or a sailboat. Or a flock of geese, since the wide-angle lens lets you see double the field of vision of conventional telescopes. The 60mm lens is distortion-free as well and has seventy-three times the light-gathering ability of the human eye, so its power is sure even under dark conditions.

Other features include a 4 × 15 finder-scope, an azimuth lock, a rubber eye shield, micro altitude control, and—if that flap you caused never dies down—a full-color Rand McNally map of outer space.

Price: $229.

Supplier: Sharper Image.

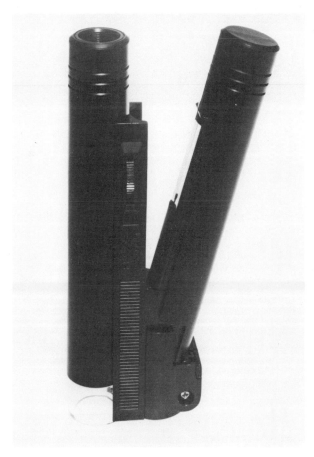

color compensation, and runs on two #ERAA batteries. Cigar-size at less than 6 by 2 by 1 inch, it fits neatly in a pocket. A leatherette carrying case is included.

Price: $24.95 (batteries, not included, are $1.75 a pair).

Supplier: Markline.

Light Scope

Is that a fly in your soup? Or is it a bug of another breed altogether? No need to befoul your fingers while finding out. Just whip out your pocket-size Panasonic microscope, unfold it to activate the built-in light, and spoon the little bugger under the lens. Magnification is thirty times actual size. So if you see hairy little legs kicking, complain to the chef. If it's circuitry that snaps into focus, yours is a complaint of an entirely different order.

Light Scope features a rack-and-pinion mechanism for smooth focus, a blue filter for

Brass Spyglass

Poohsie Hathaway has invited you to picnic aboard her yacht while you watch the regatta in Marblehead Harbor. You accept eagerly because the word throughout the agency is that Poohsie's enterprising little sister, Cissy, has opened up a concession stand on the pier, and she's selling more than souvenirs. Cissy, it seems, irked Mumsy

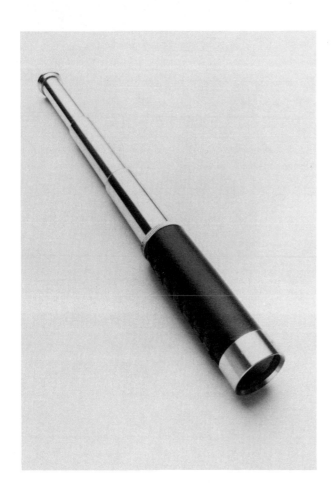

Hathaway and, in a flash of the pen, was cut out of her share of the family's fortune, every penny of which was earned by the family's patented plutonium conversion process. This explosive family secret is precisely what Cissy is peddling, the Agency suspects.

Keep an eye on Cissy; that was the order. But you know too that you must fit into these proceedings. So you pack your ever-elegant brass spyglass, to give you a stylish but always sharp look at all the action.

This Tasco Spyglass is a tiny 5 inches in length but—like an authentic ship's spyglass—it extends to a full 15 inches. Magnification is twenty-five times, and the lens is precision ground and fully coated for distortion-free viewing. Weight is 24 ounces, and the spyglass comes with a cushioned carrying case that conveniently loops to your belt for security on boats, hikes, wherever a closer eye on whatever is happening is wanted.

Price: $39.

Supplier: Sharper Image.

SCREAMS AND SHOUTS: ALARMS

NOWHERE IN THE ESPIONAGE UNIVERSE *is the technological revolution more instantly apparent than in the world of alarms: that's how dramatically they have changed in a decade or two. Twenty years ago so-called hard-wire alarms—systems that feature a wire probe on every window or entryway to be guarded—were the only choice. It was a solution that was not without flaws. Installation, for one, was laborious, expensive, and easily botched. Even when properly in place, hard-wire alarms often could be shorted with a simple snip of the home's electric-power lines. Cut off that power, and that was that for the current-powered alarm as well.*

Long-lived DC batteries started the progress. No longer were alarms dependent on vulnerable house current. Then the explosion hit: sound detectors, motion detectors, magnetic and microwave detectors, disguised detectors. The profusion is abundant enough to baffle any burglar—and anybody contemplating purchase of an alarm for home, office, or automobile.

In this guide we cannot sort all the assets and debits, all the variables and minutiae that go into making the best decision— especially since that decision will hinge strongly on your specific needs. But we can cover the basics . . . and a bit more than that.

Remember this, however: Every alarm system has its unique advantages and drawbacks. No system is perfect. And for the maximum protection, several systems are frequently used in harness.

Do you need an alarm system? Review the statistics on burglary and the results often shock. One in ten residences, for instance, will be burglarized this year. The average loss in a burglary is $650. But that's just the dollar value of stolen property. Get robbed or burglarized (and civilians know this as vividly as spies do) and there's instant but thorough demoralization. There has been an intruder in your home. *In cold print the emotions are not captured.* In reality they are. Painfully.

Voice Driver

You've set up a diamond dealership in mid-town Manhattan, and the international gossip your customers casually engage in while buying and selling rocks amply justifies the costly pains you've taken to make this operation appear fully authentic. Besides, this front is a hands-down improvement over running that bar on Corsica, so this is an assignment you intend to hold on to.

Trouble is, in addition to attracting diamond buyers, your front is also a magnet for burglars and thieves, and HQ has forcefully insisted that the least you can do is not cost the agency any more money. Just one break-in—a single stolen diamond—and your record will be in tatters. That is HQ's solemn warning.

Ha, you snort. Not get robbed in Manhattan? It's simpler to pull off a wet job in the Kremlin than to avoid theft in New York.

But you hunker down to the mission, because another stint in Corsica is not on your personal agenda. You methodically sort through the conventional security gadgets and options, and unhappily reject them all.

Sirens, bells, burglar alarms: none would work because none would draw the slightest notice in bustling, jaded midtown.

Fire: A shrill call of "fire" will bring help fast, even here. Voice Driver is the solution.

Just connect Voice Driver to any existing alarm system, and it takes care of the rest . . . all in a humanlike voice. There are two channels—one for calls of "fire, fire"; the other screams, "burglar, burglar"—and in both cases it's a microprocessor that creates the genuine-sounding voice signal.

The standard model Voice Driver is low powered but still blares out its call loud and clear, and an optional speaker can be added at any time for a more booming shout for help. The newer, more powerful unit features a self-contained 30-watt speaker system for a decibel-cracking howl.

Fine, you agree—but what if HQ quixotically ships you back to Corsica anyway? Take Voice Driver with you. Voice signals are available not only in English but also German, French, Spanish, and Dutch.

Price: Basic Model—$35.
High-Powered Speaker—$27.
Voice Driver with Built-In Speaker—$99.

Supplier: Mountain West.

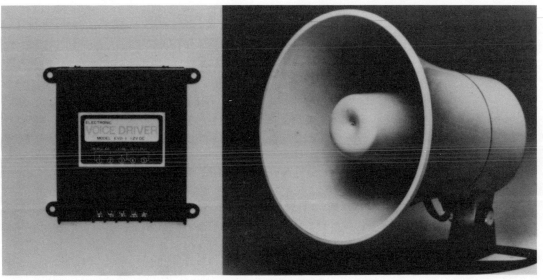

BASIC MODEL VOICE DRIVER AND HIGH-POWERED SPEAKER

Perimeter Alarm

Billy "Bad Hands" McGuire is mad and heading your way. He is not coming to shake your hand or even to spout his impassioned feelings on Ireland's northern six counties. No, Billy has sniffed out your covert negotiations with the other side, and it's his unshakable view that your "quiet diplomacy" ranks no better than double-dealing, low treachery. That's the bad news. Worse news is that Bad Hands aims to use his paws to fragment every bone in your body, and if he gets into your home, his state of mind and his bulk

ensure that he will break your head and more. He will determinedly do all this despite the screams of your intrusion detectors—because those alarms, most of them, only signal once an intruder or burglar is already inside. With Bad Hands, that will be too late.

You've got to have a distant-early-warning system, one that affords advance announcement of Bad Hand's arrival . . . and plenty of time to mount a suitably nefarious welcome, either on your own or with the help of police.

The Perimeter Alarm is designed to give that early word. Just wire it in and you have a total system for guarding doors, windows, all points of entry. At the slightest sign of attempted intrustion, the loud, 8-inch-diameter alarm bell will shriek its warning . . . *before* a burglar breaks in.

Magnetic switches on doors are a key part of the system. Put a switch in place, and whenever a door is opened, the wired circuit breaks and the alarm screeches.

On windows it's foil that does the job. A Vibration Detector enhances the safeguarding capabilities by providing an alert if there's a hard shake or vibration of a window.

Be certain to trip up Billy and like-minded fellows with the Pressure Mat. For use indoors or out, this mat is wired directly into the alarm system for truly distant early warnings. Hide it under a doormat, rug, or carpet, and when an intruder so much as gently steps on it, the entire system jumps into loud service.

PERIMETER ALARM

PRESSURE MAT

The Panic Switch is the doomsday touch. Mount it anywhere, and in an emergency just push the buttom. Alarms will howl and echo from every cranny.

Even Billy Bad Hands can't punch this system out. The alarm itself is housed in a heavy-gauge-steel box with an antitamper switch to forestall attempts at dismantling.

Power for the system is provided by a 12-volt battery, so not even a blackout puts it out of commission.

Prices: Perimeter Alarm—$99.95.
Window Foil—$5.99 per roll.
Pressure Mat—$9.95.
Vibration Detector—$3.95.
Panic Switch—$1.49.
12-Volt Battery—$10.39.

Supplier: Radio Shack.

Microprocessor Burglar Alarms

You're fed up. Not with the other side . . . not with burglars, intruders, and thugs. Make no mistake, you are sick of them, too. But right now you're drowning in a spaghetti sea of hard wires, all dangling out of your perimeter alarm system. It's a great system, you agree, but somehow it just doesn't work with your interior design.

You need an alarm that covers your home—to protect valuable papers, electronic gadgetry, yourself. A *wireless* Microprocessor-Controlled System is the solution.

Rooted deep in high-tech innovations, a Microprocessor shoots out radio-frequency energy. When this enveloping force field is disturbed, a powerful alarm blasts out its call for help, because the system "reads" the disturbance as a sure sign of an intruder. And all this happens *before* the intruder gains entry, since the system busily, reliably monitors all points of entry.

A receiver/central alarm is the system's space-age heart. Its job is to pick up the constant flow of electronic messages from tiny transmitters that are placed on doors and windows. *No* wires connect the transmitters with the central brain; communications are through the air via undetectable energy beams.

That's just the beginning of the advantages when this force is with you. With the top-of-the-line Safe House Microprocessor, for instance, there's a built-in alarm speaker and a digital "disarm" code that can be punched into the box to call off false alarms. Exit/entry delays of 5 to 45 seconds can be programmed in so that you can freely enter and leave your home without triggering the system's alarm.

SAFE HOUSE MICROPROCESSOR ALARM #1

SAFE HOUSE MICROPROCESSOR ALARM #2 PLUS DOOR TRANSMITTER

Even the lower-cost model does not arrive bare. It, too, features a built-in alarm/speaker plus a fixed 30-second exit/entry delay.

As many point-of-entry transmitters as you'd like can be added to either system. For a more potent alarm punch, there's an optional and separately mounted electronic siren. And an optional External Switcher can be fitted to the top-of-the-line system to turn lamps and lights on throughout the house whenever the central alarm is activated.

Prices: Microprocessor #1—$179.95.
Microprocessor #2—$99.95.
Extra Transmitters—$29.95 apiece.
Alarm Horns/Sirens—$19.95–39.95.
External Switcher—$34.95.

Supplier: Radio Shack.

Midex Burglar Alarm

Occam's razor, the principle that the simplest correct solution is the best, cuts in espionage as well as philosophy and mathematics. And just as a logician will cite that hoary rule as the reason for choosing a one-step explana-tion over a multistep version, you can point to it as backup for picking the Midex Burglar Alarm.

Midex, like hard-wire and microprocessor systems, covers up to 5000 cubic feet of space. But to activate Midex, just plug it into a wall outlet and hook up a pair of speakers. Midex is already on the job. There are *no* transmitters to position, no sensors to install. And that is a big plus.

Another plus is that Midex is a sophisticated, solid-state, microwave motion detector. Let an intruder enter Midex's turf, and the device angrily reacts with an earsplitting howl that's loud enough to frighten off the intruder and in the process alert the whole neighborhood to the trouble in your home.

Circuitry is designed to discriminate normal household activity, so false alarms are minimized. And a built-in entry delay allows 30 seconds to disarm the alarm. Otherwise Midex will blast for 8 minutes, shut off, and promptly reset itself for another round.

Secure digital access allows off/on switching by punching in a three-figure code to arm or disarm Midex. A four-hour standby battery is included, too, in case an intruder severs the power to your home.

For economical service, Midex may be fed into conventional stereo speakers. Add optional blast-horn speakers for a louder, more potent warning.

Prices: Midex—$199.95.
Blast horns—$39.95 apiece.

Supplier: Mountain West.

Invisible Infrared Alarm System

Manny the Mummy is not called that because of a fetish for late-night movies or an eccentric sexuality. He got his name this

way: When Manny works at his trade of burglary, he is absolutely, painstakingly soundless. His skill at silence defies all odds—and also all sound-sensitive alarms. You know all this but you recognize, too, that Manny the Mummy is hot on the trail of the fresh batch of Albanian communiqués that now rest in your office safe.

This Albanian treasure is priceless . . . but a fortune need not be spent to defend it. Not when the low-cost Invisible Infrared Alarm System will happily do the job.

A two-piece system, it includes a transmitter/receiver and a beam reflector. Once it is switched on, the transmitter/receiver tirelessly, continuously shoots an invisible and narrow beam of infrared light at the reflector, which, in turn, immediately bounces it back to the transmitter/receiver. Whenever the constant travel of the beam is interrupted, the alarm is promptly triggered. And the burglar, intruder, assailant is loudly detected.

You have a choice of alarms, too. Once triggered, at your option, the alarm will blare nonstop until manually deactivated; or it will sound only during the breaking of the beam; or during the breaking of the beam plus 10 seconds. So the device can be used not just as an intruder detector but also as a mechanical and reliable way to greet and announce visitors entering the area you designate.

Naturally, since the beam is invisible, an intruder cannot know to attempt to sidestep it. With the attached mounting bracket, the transmitter/receiver can be placed covertly high on a wall or shelf. And the two component units can be as far apart as 50 feet, which enables the device to monitor a wide area thoroughly.

An LED test/alignment indicator is built in, as is a buzzer alarm. Connections can also be made to optional bells and sirens for a more blaring announcement.

Price: $69.95 ($21.95 for an optional 8″ Alarm Bell; $19.95 for an Electronic Siren).

Supplier: Radio Shack.

The Informer

You have a Gutenberg in your library. While the entirety of the estate is secured like a fortress, you want, always, to be well aware of the doings around your books. That's why you install the Informer.

In just two evenings you can easily build this ultrasonic sensor, which looks like a book for effective blending amid your priceless first editions. Once in place, the Informer does not make for fascinating reading—but it is ever alert to all movements within 25 feet. When it detects the slightest sound, it will, at your option, turn on a light, buzz a buzzer, set off a siren, or roar an alarm. You build it, so the choice of which electrical device the Informer activates is wholly yours.

But Gutenberg protection is not the Informer's only role. Its innocuous disguise allows it to be installed anywhere in a home. Once it is on the job, the Informer silently erects a monitoring "field"; then no matter if it's a wandering child or an enemy agent who breaks the field, the Informer can be counted on to roar the news.

No special tools are required to construct the Informer, and the kit supplies all parts plus simple instructions.

Price: $59.95 ($10.95 for a buzzer-alarm accessory; $29.95 for an alarm bell).

Supplier: Heathkit.

Dial & Coder

You suspect your assistant of double-dealing. Word is, he's been bought off by the other side's Max Bakunin, who has plotted for decades to get a clear shot at rummaging through your files. Now the assistant may have delivered that dream by supplying Bakunin with keys to your office plus advance word on when your next day off is.

You cannot permit Bakunin this free access; that's obvious. But what if all this is just another paranoid fantasy, the kind that breeds fast in an agency's tense corridors? You don't want to hang around the office in a vain wait. But what if Bakunin never shows?

With the Dial & Coder, you needn't be there but you can still hear exactly what's going on. As soon as the triggering alarm is tripped, this emergency device will instantly dial your phone number (or any number that's programmed into it, including the police or a guard service), and the attached microphone will pick up all sounds in its vicinity, so you can listen in directly. That way you have the audio information you

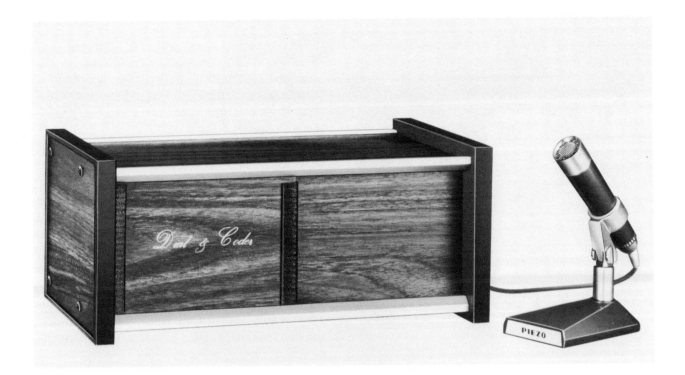

need to make a rapid decision about precisely what is happening at the office (or your apartment, vacation home—wherever you've installed Dial & Coder).

If Bakunin—or anybody else, for that matter—is at the site, you'll know with Dial & Coder. And if he arrives while you're on the line already, Dial & Coder will persist in dialing your number, speedily and automatically, until its warning call gets through. The device can't be put out of commission when electric lines are down; it runs on four 9-volt batteries for a secure power source.

What's more, you'll know Dial & Coder will operate perfectly, since you get to build it yourself with this complete kit. Detailed, understandable instructions are provided along with all parts. Extra, personal phone consultation is also available free of charge if you get stuck.

Price: $179.95.

Supplier: Heathkit.

BurglarMist

There are few unblemished records in this line of work. BurglarMist owns one of them. It has *never* failed to drive away intruders, the manufacturer proudly reports.

Take most such claims with the proverbial grain or three of salt. But BurglarMist is different. Its promise is powerfully backed by a huge, numbing, four-ounce dose of tear gas—ample to thwart nearly all intruders. Besides, once saturated with BurglarMist's nontoxic CN gas, they will be in no mood to steal or maim. They'll be far too busy coughing, hacking, and crying. A fast shower will be uppermost among their priorities.

The real advantage of BurglarMist is that it puts intruders out of commission immediately and directly. Most warning devices (alarms, for instance) can offer only secondary protection because they only summon help—which will take, at best, several minutes to arrive at the scene.

Activation of BurglarMist is by a self-contained mechanical trip wire (which responds to a slight 5-ounce pull); or the device

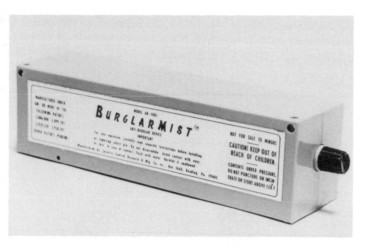

can be integrated into a standard alarm system for triggering whenever the alarm is set off. In both cases BurglarMist's direction nozzle is adjustable for accurate coverage of any area up to 2000 square feet.

A time-delay model also allows for a pause of 20 seconds after activation before BurglarMist shoots out its gas to allow for safe entry into the guarded premises by those who know precisely how to disarm the device's safety pin. That's easily accomplished. But not by an intruder who's unaware of BurglarMist's lurking presence.

Prices: Base Model—$35.
Time Delay Model—$70.

Supplier: Mountain West.

Infrared Outdoor Motion Detector

Nancy. A nice name. But the Nancy who is pursuing you is not nice at all. She's from the other side and a bona fide ninja master to boot, so her forte is dark, deadly stealth. Dressed all in black and more silent than a cat, Nancy's lethal successes are legion, because you cannot thwart what you cannot see, and Nancy, when she works, is close to invisible.

Throw a revealing light on her and all other intruders with an Infrared Outdoor Motion Detector, which responds to the slightest movement by flicking on a flood of illumination. Install it anywhere outside—near the front door, the garage, in the yard—it's weatherized for durability and long, reliable performance. Once it's on the job, the detector sweeps any assigned area (up to 25 × 35 feet) with its sensitive infrared rays . . . and whenever those invisible rays are disturbed, the device unhesitatingly activates a connected floodlight and the area is bathed in enough light to promptly scare off virtually all uninvited guests. The lights will stay on for a full four minutes, to give you time to investigate safely. When the four minutes are up, the light automatically snaps off and the device resets itself and again goes on the alert for new signs of motion.

(A photoelectric switch is built in to shut the device off during daylight hours.)

But which light should you throw on your potentially deadly visitors? Any standard 120-volt AC light can be connected in tandem with the Infrared Detector. For brilliant

but inexpensive light, for instance, there's the Economy Rotating Unit, which delivers ninety flashes of bright light per minute. Or for surer glare, use a Strobe Light—sixty flashes of brilliant, pulsing-red illumination per minute.

Prices: Infrared Detector—$199.
Economy Rotating Light—$80.
Strobe Light—$189.

(Note: The Economy Rotating Light also works when plugged into a car's cigarette lighter, to give you extra applications.)

Supplier: Mountain West.

Mobile Alert

The meet is at the Beverly Wilshire Hotel and you're in luck. A parking space beckons, and it's legal. That's essential, both because your motto is to draw no undue attention to yourself, ever (all spies live by that motto, and illegal parking, though seemingly a minor matter, blatantly invites notice) and, more to the present point, you'll need the car handy for the quick escape that will be the last act of this present piece of work.

You briskly but with measured pace march into the El Padrino Room and prepare for the wait. The mark will show in his good time. There's no rushing that.

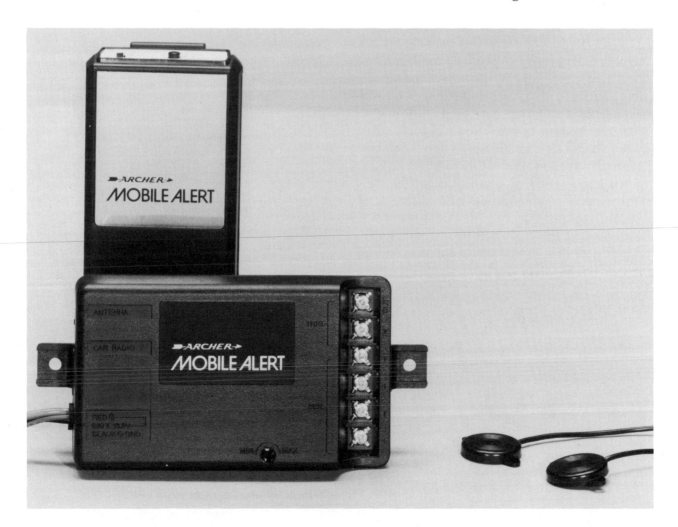

Beep, beep, beep. The small alert sounds from your breast pocket.

It was a setup all along. Somebody is tampering with your car. Disabling it or, more likely, wiring a bomb into the ignition.

But you have time to gauge your response—time the opposition does not know you have. Because you know they are manhandling your car but they do *not* know you know.

That's the edge Mobile Alert (4¼ × 2¾ × 1¼ inches) delivers. It's a silent security alarm—one that does not sound at your vehicle but instead alerts only you that there are shenanigans afoot. Just mount the transmitter under the dash and connect it to the existing antenna. Attach the electronic sensors to the doors, hood, trunk . . . then wherever you are, up to half a mile away from the car, the portable receiver (4 × 2 × 1 inch) will quietly alert you to any attempted intrusion.

Hear the alert and it's up to you to call the police. But that ranks as a huge improvement over siren-type car alarms since all too often their warning shrieks go unnoticed and unreported no matter how loud their bleat. With this system you will know if your car is under siege—and you'll know, too, that the police are on the way.

An ounce of extra protection can be gotten by installation of an optional Movement Sensor Switch. Put this device under the hood, hook it up to Mobile Alert, and it will trigger a swift alert in the event your car is towed, jacked, or just jostled.

MOVEMENT SENSOR SWITCH

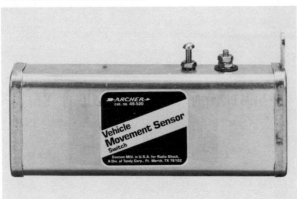

Prices: Mobile Alert—$99.95.
Movement Sensor Switch—$4.99.

Supplier: Radio Shack.

Vehicle Detector

Survive in the espionage trade long enough and the realization dawns that there are no absolutes. A chronic epistemological perversity is at work, and assets are simultaneously debits; pluses can be counted on to have a minus side. Like that long driveway that separates your country mansion from the street . . . At first blush you did joyful cartwheels at the warm security promised by a mile-long private roadway between you and the public thoroughfare. Then it occurred to you—the very length of the drive meant you

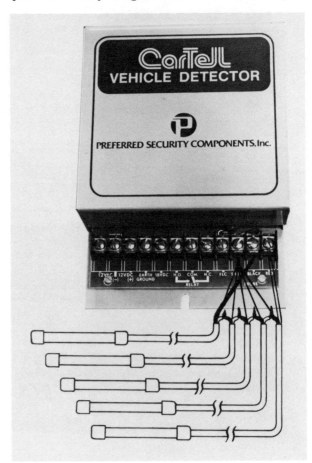

could not closely monitor comings and goings—at least not with your eyes and ears—because there is just too much territory to cover.

But the Vehicle Detector System will do what your eyes and ears cannot. Its operating principle is buried deep in sophisticated science, but in barest form what the Vehicle Detector does is monitor the earth's magnetic field—and the approach of any mass of metal, such as a car or truck, causes that field to warp. The Vehicle Detector senses the change, and its alarm sounds.

Just pick a point that warrants keen monitoring and put the system's electronic probe about six inches below the ground surface. Run the wire relay to the central unit in your home, and the system is set to go. For more protection extras probes may be added; and an electronic floodlight, with 800 watts of illumination, may be added as well. So when the next vehicle rolls by, it will promptly be bathed in light and greeted by an alarm, to make sure you are never caught by surprise.

The system is weatherproofed to minimize false alarms. One hundred feet of connecting wire comes in the package.

Prices: Vehicle Detector System—$229.
Extra Probe—$80.
Floodlight Control—$135.

Supplier: Mountain West.

Door Alarm

The travel is what wears an espionage agent down: the dreariness, even the spooky strangeness of an endless procession of lookalike hotel rooms. In none is there restful sleep, because there is no denying that the typically flimsy locks on hotel-room doors offer scant protection. A spy would pay a fortune for just one good night's sleep.

There is no need to ante up that fortune,

however. If an inexpensive, portable burglar alarm system is needed, this hooklike Door Alarm is the answer. Ideal for spies (and business travelers, too), it's only 4 inches in diameter and quickly connects—and just as rapidly disconnects—to any door without the use of tools. But let an intruder or a burglar enter its electronic detection field, and the alarm belts out an earsplitting 85-decibel shriek for as long as the intruder remains within the field.

Hands, keys, lock-picking tools—all set off the alarm, and the sensitive protection field guards the immediate area of and around the doorknob from invaders. Nor will false alarms interrupt your rest: The instrument's sensitivity is adjustable to prevent those needless disturbances and to provide warning only in the event of true emergencies.

Available only in brown, the alarm is powered by a conventional 9-volt alkaline battery. Replacement power sources are readily available, even in limited hotel shops.

Price: $29.95.

Supplier: Mountain West.

Wedge Alarm

Only a door without a lock separates you from them. You must always know their whereabouts, but they must not discover you while you're busy eating the evidence of your mission. It is with frantic dismay that you notice: not only does the door lack a lock, it does not even have a knob. There is *nothing* to hang your portable door alarm on.

The Wedge Alarm was made for this moment. It's a doorstop, so it will block the door from opening. But it does double duty—let anyone try to force the door, and Wedge Alarm's siren shrilly shrieks its unhappiness at the intrusion.

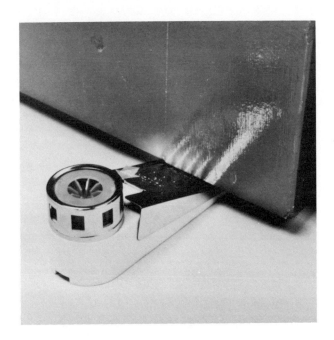

Wedge Alarm operates on two ordinary penlight batteries; its bottom is rippled to afford sure footing and eliminate sliding on tiles, concrete, or rugs. Wedged under any door—in an apartment, motel, store—it will bark out its anger when moved. And the sound is piercing enough to discourage most intruders.

Price: $5.95.

Supplier: The Peterzell Co.

Screech Alarm

Throughout the long transoceanic flight you squeezed the suitcase tighter than a miser hugs his wallet. Stewards stared; other passengers grumbled. But you insisted: The suitcase stayed at your side, mile after mile. It was worth the flight; it was all worth it, you decide, as the plane taxis into Dulles Airport. Langley, and the Company HQ, are just a hop away.

In the crowded lobby you dash fast to a pay telephone. Drop a dime and . . . drat! The suitcase and its stolen Soviet documents won't fit into the phone booth while you make the call. And it will not do to leave the suitcase unprotected outside the booth. That risk cannot be taken—you've fought for too long.

But you know the solution. Using the swatch of Velcro that comes with the Screech Alarm, just attach this portable device to your suitcase and pull out the pin. If anyone so much as accidentally jostles the suitcase now, the alarm will let rip 110 tooth-rattling decibels of screeching—and it will not cease its howl until the pin is reinserted.

The big noise is always produced, even though the alarm itself is tiny ($4^3/8 \times 2^3/8 \times 1^5/8$ inches) for complete portability. And with the handy Velcro strip, it can be attached to nearly anything. Then if it's disturbed, as the supplier promises, it will "scream bloody murder!"

Price: $32.95.

Supplier: Brookstone.

AudioLite

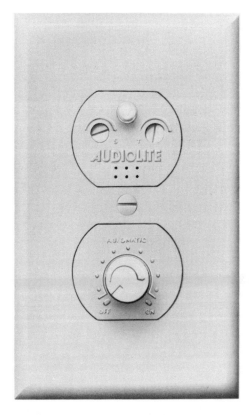

Fionnula Feline—That's the sobriquet of the East's most adept cat burglar—is on your case. Word is, she's the advance man. Her sole task is to case your penthouse at night; learn every corner, every hiding place. Only later will her employer show—once he's mulled over her insights and room plans— and it is then that the other side's homicidal intent will be revealed.

Fionnula cannot be allowed to escape with her information. But preventing that is the trick. Her m.o. is well known: She works only at night and dresses all in black, and nobody knows her true appearance. She's an expert, too, at dismantling alarms, picking locks, and outwitting hidden cameras, and she invariably leaves a room exactly as she found it so nobody is ever sure if in fact she's been there.

You've got a plan, however—but it better work. You know what rides on it.

So you brazenly, conspicuously opt for a night on the town. Dressed in a black tuxedo, you march out of your building . . . but cautiously, cleverly circle around to the building directly across from yours. You hop up to the thirteenth floor, where you'll be on direct eye level with your penthouse, and now you wait.

But not long. Voilà! Someone's within your apartment. You know because there's a light blazing in your living room. A figure dressed in black dashes to the bedroom to escape. Ha! Lights flash on in that room— and in every room Fionnula enters until, desperate, she bolts onto the balcony for a panicked departure. There, too, the light goes on and you get a last good look at Ms. Feline, the now-declawed cat burgler.

Yes, quiet a good cat burglar is . . . but not still enough to fool AudioLite, an ingenious light switch that turns on lights whenever it hears a sound. Its built-in sound sensor is sensitive enough to hear small tinkles but can be adjusted to respond to any level of noise you'd like, from a whisper to a shout and sounds in between. Once the audio threshold level is crossed and the lights are triggered on, they'll stay on for the time you also pick, from seven seconds to seven minutes. What's more, since AudioLite resets itself whenever it hears a new sound, it will keep the lights on for as long as there is any noise at all.

AudioLite replaces conventional light switches in a few minutes. Only a screwdriver is needed to do the job, and the device works with any incandescent light up to 300 watts.

AudioLite is handy for more than detecting cat burglars. It can be counted on to snap on the lights whenever anybody enters a room where it's on the job. So if an intruder enters, he is sure to be bathed in unwelcome illumination. Or if it's you who comes home late with your arms laden with groceries, again AudioLite will be there to welcome you and show the way in.

Price: $34 ($99 for four).

Supplier: Sharper Image.

BANNING THE BOMB: EXPLOSIVE SNIFFERS AND METAL DETECTORS

IT IS NO SECRET: *Bombs are easily fabricated by amateurs. The ingredients—common chemicals—can be bought, usually for pennies, at any chemical or pharmaceutical supply house. The transaction is legal.*

Legal, too, are instructional books and pamphlets with to-the-point titles like How to Make a Mortar *and* Plastique Explosive in Your Bathtub. *The assembly is simple; the results are deadly.*

Ever since the 1960s bombing has emerged as a major political sport. Played most earnestly in Europe and the Middle East, it's also taken a toll in the United States: the Mobil Oil building in New York and the Capitol in Washington, D.C., are just two locations on the lengthening list.

Most certainly spies cannot shrug off the threat of bombs. A few years back, for instance, the B. R. Fox Company circulated its "classified" catalog of ASTRO tools and equipment. Prominently featured were: a telephone headset bomb, a flashlight rigged to explode when moved, a booby-trapped M-16 ammo clip, and a bomb hidden in a cigarette pack.

Orlando Letelier, an exiled Chilean intellectual and politician, found out the final and hard way that space-age explosives are not confined to James Bond movies and esoteric compendia. One morning Letelier was motoring along a bustling District of Columbia street. Somewhere up ahead, a button was pushed, and in an instant his car burst into a shower of metallic rain. The Chilean met instant death as a result of the high-tech radio-controlled bomb that had been concealed in his car.

Businesswomen and men, diplomats, journalists, even innocent and uninvolved passersby (like the 86 Italians who died in the recent Fascist bombing of a Bologna train station) are not immune. Terror is part of every bombing. The sloppiness of the kill, of the destruction is purposeful: It spreads the message more forcefully.

That, perhaps, is why spies rarely use bombs on each other: It would disrupt the privacy of the international game. Nevertheless, the rules are not always observed. They are *tacit and may be broken*—as an Israeli hit team did in its bombing murders of twenty plus Palestinian agents in retaliation for the Black September's massacre of Israeli athletes at the Munich Olympics.

All of which explains why there has been an explosion—a beneficial one—in technologies designed to find bombs before *they* find us.

Acousti-Sensor

Every time Whiny Warner calls, disaster strikes. And now he's left his adenoidal message on your answering machine: "Hickory, dickory, dock. The bomb's a ticking clock. When it strikes one, you'd better run, or it's at the pearly gates you'll knock." It's not just his lousy poetry that drives you nuts, but his uncanny lack of specificity. Where the hell is the bomb? In your car . . . house . . . somewhere on the grounds? And does he mean one a.m. or p.m.? In any case, there's no time to waste.

What you need are ultrasensitive ears, since 90 percent and more of all bombs are detonated by timing devices. If only you could hear the relentless tick, tick, tick, you could pinpoint the bomb's location and swiftly implement appropriate deactivation procedures.

The Acousti-Sensor provides those ears.

Listen to the near-silent ticking of your wristwatch. The sound is barely audible. Introduce a watch to Acoustic-Sensor, however, and those ticks are amplified a thousand times—to levels high enough to allow for easy location and detection of any dangerous timing devices in your vicinity. Operating on 9-volt batteries, Acousti-Sensor is portable, too, and in perilously tight situations can be used remotely in conjunction with connection cables that permit an effective broadcast range of two miles.

The Acousti-Sensor need not be operated only for bomb detection. It's a versatile device that can be adjusted to amplify any vibratory or vocal noise and, consequently, can be employed in overhearing distant conversations, too.

Earphones are included for clarity and privacy.

Price: $695.

Supplier: LEA.

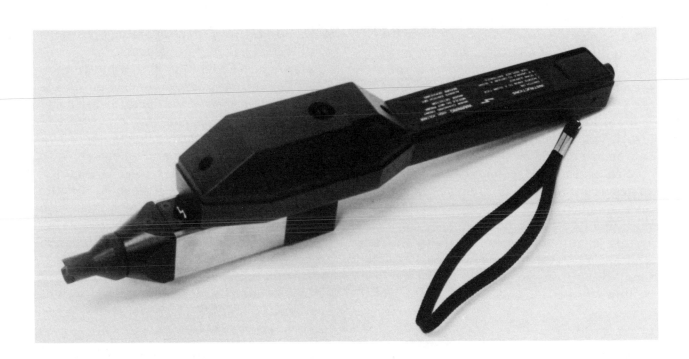

Bomb Spy

In 1980 the president of United Airlines was at home, reading his mail. Until he opened one more letter. That one contained the letter bomb that was potent enough to maim him seriously.

That executive was lucky—he lived. Not so PLO official Mahmoud Hamchari, who, in 1973, was staying in a Paris hotel and enjoying a bout of afternoon sex. The phone rang. Hamchari answered. He identified himself to the caller. The bomb hidden in Hamchari's telephone exploded; his death was instantaneous.

Bombs come in all sizes, all shapes. A fatal charge can be as small as a cube of sugar, as flat as a letter, as harmless-looking as a cigar. And they can all be killers, because technology has made packaging a bomb in nearly any form feasible—and lethal.

But technology also created the Bomb Spy. It's made to detect hidden dangers and to enable you to respond before it's too late. A portable, hand-held system, Bomb Spy sniffs out a bomb's characteristic vapor—the invisible, telltale scent all explosives emit no matter what their guise. If suspicious gases are present, Bomb Spy's warning light immediately goes on, and an audible tone quickly follows. Total time elapsed? One second (and just two minutes are needed for Bomb Spy to be warmed up and on the job).

Bad news? You've found a bomb? Best advice is to vacate the premises fast. And *then* summon technical assistance. Do all this rapidly because Bomb Spy's dual alert system is crafted to screen out false alarms. And the full system is continuously monitored by built-in circuitry to guard against malfunctions.

Price: $2000.

Supplier: CCS.

Explosive Vapor Detector

Your nose crinkles, and suddenly you're yelling, "Out! There's a bomb. A *bomb!*" Co-workers stare at you in befuddled, wary dismay. But you know what you're talking about. Bombs not only kill, they smell. Even the ones that don't include a ticking clock or a radio receiver in their innards still emit a steady and detectable vapor. No human nose, unfortunately, is finely attuned enough to pounce on that warning odor. But the Model 70 Explosives Detector is.

Created for personnel screening, airport security, mailroom monitoring, and all-purpose threat-search applications and built in accordance with US government and North Atlantic Treaty Organization (NATO) specifications, Model 70 features a unique and highly sensitive twin electron detector system that will react dependably even to vapor concentrations as scant as one part per *billion* parts of air; and its operating spectrum is wide enough to sniff the gamut of commercial and military explosives compositions while still rejecting false alarms.

Battery powered (and with a built-in automobile battery–adaptor connection for extended and intensive field operations), Model 70 needs just 1½ seconds in the presence of explosives vapors before it signals the warning on its visual display and follows up with an audio alarm. Only 1 second is required afterward for Model 70 to clear its circuits and be fully prepared for a fresh bout with suspected vapors.

Crafted for portability, Model 70's search probe weighs just 7 pounds. The support unit, including a self-contained battery pack (with 3½ hours of operating power) weighs another 25 pounds.

Price: $11,280.

Supplier: Ion Track Instruments (ITI).

Entry-Scan

It's a meeting, a convention . . . and your aim is a truce among the battling parties. Just wishful thinking? You hope not; international peace rests on your success. But you're not trusting to hope alone. Bring those pugnacious, bellicose, embittered sides into a single room and there's no telling what armaments any one of the combatants will be packing. But your big worry, especially in this group, is a walking time bomb, a suicide who is ready to die in an explosive flash as long as he gets the satisfaction of slaughtering everybody in the room in the flaming process.

Farfetched? You know it's not. Not when you're dealing with terrorists. And you're familiar with the dozens of airplane hijackings masterminded and devised by willing human bombs.

But you see the hitch when you review security options. The meeting will be attended by politicians, diplomats, people whom you cannot frisk or pat down. None will tolerate the implied slight.

Yet you cannot stand the slight of a different, killing kind that a bomb explosion would mean. So you turn to the ever-polite but thoroughly efficient Entry-Scan.

Made for installation at the entrance to any high-risk building (nuclear plants, military bases, airports, spy shops, and sensitive commercial operations are especially apt), Entry-Scan automatically but decorously screens every passer-through for telltale explosive vapors. Argon gas is the operative detector, and if the air contains just the slenderest trace of explosives vapor, a visual warning is promptly provided. Only 1½ seconds are required for Entry-Scan to make the identification, and sensitive circuitry is crafted to weed out false alarms.

Movable from location to location, Entry-Scan (which in appearance is not unlike air-port metal detectors and can be used in tandem with them) weighs 380 pounds and measures 68 by 27½ by 17½ inches. A small Remote Operational Monitoring Unit is hooked up to it via a 5-meter cable to give a guard a second, closer look at Entry-Scan's signals. And extension cables are available for system operation from a distant guard station.

Price: $20,904.

Supplier: Ion Track Instruments (ITI).

Nuke Spooker

You sense a trap. Too easily, you've found the secret hideout of an international band of terrorists. What's up? The radiation level, you find as you turn on your Nuke Spooker. Faint at first, the alarm loudens as you step toward the door. When you back away, the sound fades, the alarm lights dim. Chock-full of information or not, this is one den of such deadly iniquity you decide to postpone your visit until you are properly attired—in a lead suit.

Whether the nuclear waste was produced by errant terrorists or misbehaving militarists, the Nuke Spooker instantly warns of

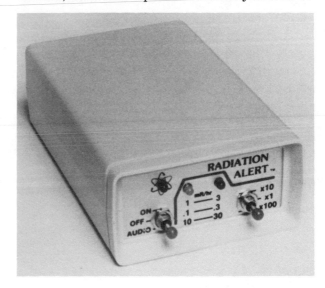

its presence . . . at the landfill next door, from a leaky microwave, or in a glass of milk from Three Mile Island. It does this reliably, because Nuke Spooker works on a proven Geiger-counter-style principle. Its audio alarm in conjunction with visual signals will lead you to (or away from) any nearby radiation. Sensitivity is built into the mechanism to sidestep false alarms.

A solid-state system, Nuke Spooker is small enough to be carried in a pocket, purse, briefcase, or car glove compartment.

Price: $907.

Supplier: CCS.

The Safety Circle

It's too late: The bomb *will* explode, and you've resignedly called off attempts to defuse it. Even so, the bomb's explosive impact must be minimized—many lives are at stake.

Wall the bomb in with Safety Circle. Its multilayers of ballistic nylon provide reliable side support against explosions. And to make sure this bomb is effectively encircled, Safety Circle is 6 feet high and 72 feet long (which translates into a circle that's 15 feet in diameter).

Add more protection by smothering the bomb with Bomb Blanket, 4 feet by 4 feet of heavy-duty, reinforced ballistic nylon (35 pounds' worth in all).

Or, if it's a letter bomb, quick—shove it in a Letterbomb Pouch: a 17-by-17-inch and 18-pound self-contained pouch that's designed to afford safe storage while a bomb is transported to safer, less sensitive grounds.

Prices: Safety Circle—$100.
Bomb Blanket—$310.
Letterbomb Pouch—$450.

Supplier: LEA.

Bomb Ranger

It happens again and again: The executive, politician, or spy climbs into his car for the morning ride to the office. He is not incautious, however, so before starting the vehicle he meticulously checks for telltale signs of a bomb. His relief comes out in a sigh when all's safe, and he starts the car. His breath is momentarily heavy once more, but again nothing happens, and he smilingly drives off.

Bamm! Two blocks down the road the terrorist-planted bomb rips through the car. The automobile is demolished; the target, killed.

There would be a markedly different ending to that story if the target had owned Bomb Ranger. Here is what it would have sounded like: *Bamm!* The bomb explodes. But the target's smile broadens. Because Bomb Ranger is made to explode all bombs long before *you* get there.

Bomb Ranger's mandate is to search out and explode all radio-controlled explosives and to do this far in advance of your arrival

on the scene. Its scanner is involved in a nonstop probe of all radio frequencies in a radius of up to one kilometer, and that means you have a half-mile of safe breathing room.

But there's a pair of hitches with Bomb Ranger, good as the device is. For one, it can find and detonate *only* radio-controlled bombs, ones that are detonated by remote control. Yet that's how most such bombs work, and with Bomb Ranger you may not have total security but you have picked up a sizable margin of self-defense for your side.

The other worry is less dismissable. Roll back to the story of the foiled bomb. Note that Bomb Ranger does not deactivate explosives—it prematurely *detonates* them. With a thorough disregard for whatever bystanders happen to be in the vicinity.

Not surprisingly, Bomb Ranger is not legally licensable for use in the United States. It is in common use, however, in many Latin American, Middle Eastern, and European nations.

Price: $160,000.

Supplier: CCS.

SAFETY FIRST: SECURING YOUR SECRETS

ONCE UPON A TIME, *the fairy tale will begin, houses and offices were left unlocked twenty-four hours a day. Tell that to the next generation and there will be disbelieving laughter. Nowadays even churches are locked around the clock.*

No, neither the best door lock nor the best safe will keep every intruder out. There's never a guarantee. Ask the Brinks Company, which, in the 1950 Boston robbery, lost $2.7 million to a ragtag gang of thieves. The burglars had concocted plans for blowing the Brinks vault, but that wasn't necessary. The exterior doors to the Brinks building were unlocked; the vault itself was wide open. And in the absence of enforced security precautions, this mini mob waltzed in and out with their record-breaking haul in a matter of minutes.

The evidence left behind was so scanty that the gang was ultimately arrested and convicted only when one of the members, an inveterate smalltime crook, was later arrested for shoplifting in Pennsylvania. The FBI suspected the group but could prove nothing until this minor arrest provided the leverage needed to pry out a confession. Faced with a sprawling list of indictments—larceny, lewd conduct, illegal possession of weapons—the petty thief traded testimony against his fellow gang members for a lesser sentence. But the loot, incidentally, was never recovered, and the thieves eventually made a lucrative sale of their story to Hollywood: The Great Brinks Job, *starring Peter Falk, was the upshot. The movie flopped . . . which may say something about how and when crime pays.*

The point, of course, is that the best security equipment will not work if it is not used. Buy good locks—and lock them. If you install a safe, yes, it's a nuisance, but put your valuables in it. When you purchase a paper shredder, run every sheet through it. Do all that and the other side will never know what it's missing . . . but that precisely is the point.

Electronic Doorlock System

A curious schizophrenia afflicts many spies. Masters of detail at work, at home they're forever baffled by the tiniest matters. And not infrequently locked out of their own houses because, somehow, the door key was left behind at the Dulles Airport X-ray scanner. So a locksmith must be summoned hurriedly, both to get into the home and to change *all* the locks, because who knows what hands that key may have fallen into.

Free yourself from the tyranny of keys forever: Install an Electronic Doorlock system. Operating much like a bank's automatic teller, the virtually pickproof Electronic Doorlock features a stainless-steel keyboard

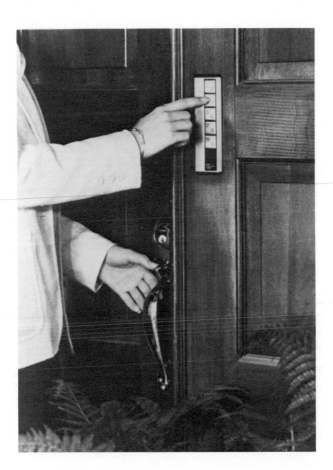

into which you punch the "open sesame" code you previously programmed into the machine's memory. The code tickles the lock's innards, and bingo, the door swings open.

The combination can be conveniently changed at any time, and for special occasions a second combination can be programmed in to provide temporary access for friends, neighbors, visiting relatives—and you can erase that code just by pressing a few buttons. A would-be intruder can't gain entry simply by randomly pressing digits until he scores. After sixteen wrong entries are pushed, an antitamper feature swings into action and shuts down the keyboard for twenty-five seconds.

With no moving parts, the battery-operated system is durable and is designed to withstand extremes of weather as well as vandalism. Installation is fast; there's no wiring involved. All necessary elements come with the package, and the keyless electronic system readily interfaces with existing door hardware.

Price: $109.

Supplier: Mountain West.

Fire and Explosion-Resistant Safes

You've been entrusted with deciphering the encrypted Argentine martial messages, and you are aware that skilled, prompt work will win you that promotion you've long coveted. So you're laboring around the clock on this assignment, both at the office and at home. You know you cannot relax your guard over the documents; lose even one tiny microdot and that's that, not just for the promotion but for your job (and—you tremble at the suggestion—perhaps your life as well). Nor would it matter to HQ how that microdot was lost: theft, intrusion, fire, explosion, violent acts of nature . . . save your breath. No excuse will be accepted. And that means you've got to provide ever-vigilant, continuing protection for these sensitive piles of papers. Try as you might, however, there's no cramming those priceless reams into the array of mini-safes (phony wall outlets, dummy books, hollow photograph stands) that you've scattered around your house for stowing jewels, loose cash, and other small valuables. What you need is a big safe for big protection.

There's the Sentry File Chest for starters—it's spacious enough to swallow .86 cubic feet of goodies, and it's made to keep them secure. A tough key lock thwarts intruders, plus the cement-compound insulated walls provide protection against fire (up to 350 degrees) for one hour. Explosions, too, are resisted because (in a standard industry test) this safe can take being hurled abruptly into a 2000-degree furnace with no resulting damage to its contents. Despite all that safety, this safe's base weight is 70 pounds. And a removable steel tray for keeping small valuables secure but handy is included.

Want to give intruders a still more baffling foe? Move up to the Sentry Floor Safe—

SENTRY SAFE

400 pounds of heavy-gauge steel, insulated walls, interlocking body and door jambs, and a recessed combination lock. Capacity is 4.5 cubic feet, and this rugged safe can also withstand explosions and protect its contents for up to two hours against 350-degree heat. Its durability is proven, too, since the Sentry Floor Safe passes the cruel "impact" test—a remorseless trial that requires a candidate to first live through fire, which is followed by a thirty-foot drop onto crushed brick or concrete, then yet another round of fire is administered. To pass, the safe's contents must survive this ordeal. That's exactly what the Sentry Safe delivers.

Or maybe yours is that critical storage and security need that can only be handled by an industrial-type floor safe, one that's operated by a combination lock and passes with ease the fire, explosion, and impact tests. With a separate, key-operated interior compartment for an extra measure of safety and an anti-intruder feature that activates a deadbolt whenever there's tampering, plus three steel bolts for a secure lock-up of the safe's contents, you're in luck. And you have many models to choose from:

- Model 6595 holds 3.3 cubic feet and can take 350 degrees for two hours. It weighs 350 pounds.

- Model 6597 holds 5.2 cubic feet and withstands 350 degrees for one hour. It weighs in at 335 pounds.

- Model 6594 survives 350 degrees for one hour and holds 7.9 cubic feet. It tips the scales at 670 pounds.

- Model 6591 grants 350-degree/one-hour protection for its 11.6 cubic feet of stored valuables. At 790 pounds, it's a heavyweight. But its big brother (Model 6522, not pictured) dwarfs it. The big brother delivers *four* hours of 350-degree protection with its 1455 pounds of steel . . . a hefty combination that makes it tops in safekeeping.

Prices: Sentry File Chest $99.
Sentry Safe $535.
Model 6595 $1015.
Model 6597 $1050.
Model 6594 $1370.
Model 6591 $1620.
Model 6522 $2150.

Supplier: Sears.

The Safe That Hides Itself

Dierdre Deftfinger is on your case again. You've got the negatives, she wants them, and in her presence there is no such thing as an uncrackable safe. Where do you hide the precious celluloid? In Secure-All-Safe, the safe that hides itself. After all, ace jim-crack though she is, if Ms. Deftfinger can't find it, she can't crack it.

A top quality wall safe, Secure-All-Safe has an important asset: It's made to close flush with the wall, so it can be hidden not only by the somewhat obvious framed painting, but also by a thin sheet of wallpaper. There are no telltale bumps.

Even if the Secure-All-Safe is spotted, it's not an easy mark. The steel is heavy gauge; the hinge is covered and runs the length of the door; there are double, interlocking door edges; a rugged key-opened lock; and high-temperature insulation as well as water-proofing for protection of valuables in fire, flood, and other disasters.

The safe's interior includes a compartment for papers ($11\frac{1}{2}'' \times 11\frac{1}{2}'' \times 2''$) and a jewelry tray ($10\frac{1}{2}'' \times 1\frac{1}{8}'' \times 2''$). Its total exterior dimensions ($16\frac{7}{16}''$ wide, $17\frac{3}{8}''$ high, $4\frac{3}{8}''$ deep) allow for ready installation in any standard wall.

Price: $100 (installation not included).

Supplier: On Guard Enterprises.

Wall Outlet Safe

"You wanted it. Here it is," the defeated man numbly curses as he hurls the glimmering mountain of a diamond at your feet. Then he exits, and you are left with the prize you long contested for—plus a problem. It's Friday night, and you've got a rendezvous downtown. But it would be uncharacteristically and insanely incautious of you to leave the house with the diamond out in the open. Your wall safe won't do. At the moment it's hidden behind a dead give-away: a painting of Whistler's Mother. It's the first place they'd look.

Put the rock in a wall *outlet* safe and worry no more. Even if the intruder suspects that that's your game, the sheer number of outlets in your home will foil him because he'd never have the time to investigate that many possibilities.

Odds are, however, no burglar will be savvy to this trick. It's an authentic-looking wall outlet, minus the electrical innards and has a 7-inch-high by 2¾-inch-deep-by-2-inch-wide container for secure hiding of jewels, rolls of cash, small valuables of all kinds. Just pop the goodies inside and they'll be there when you return. Because only you have the plastic key that unlocks this mini-treasure chest.

Installation takes just minutes, and the outlet can be put into any wall of plaster, wall board, or panel. A standard ivory cover plate is provided; other colors are available to match your decor.

Price: $14.95.

Supplier: Brookstone.

Picture Safe

The problem is not in the field; it's in the home office. There's a mole loose, and he is no burrowing animal. Not this species. He's an agent for the other side, and his covert mission is to pocket your every piece of evidence. Nothing is safe on your desk. It's gotten to the exasperating point where it's not just classified documents that disappear but also

PICTURE SAFE

loose change, pipe tools, stamps, anything that's not nailed down.

Complaints to security are bootless. This mole is a clever critter—a sad fact you invariably discover when you return to your desk after an absence—even a brief one like a trip to the water cooler.

Your anger mounts. Your trust nears a nadir. Your frustration approaches volcanic levels. Volatile, violent action threatens. Until you remember your loved ones—and the idea clicks into focus as sharp as a clear picture. Because protection is a photograph away.

The Picture Safe is the weapon to deploy in this war of nerves, whether your enemy is the other side or plain petty thieves. *Nobody* will steal your family portraits, and that is the starting point. But the Picture Safe goes a clever and large step forward: It provides security behind the photographs that no robber wants.

It's an all-wood frame with a difference: Beneath the standard 5-by-7-inch photograph it displays is a secret compartment large enough (1″ in depth, 4½″ in width, and 6½″ in height) to provide 29 cubic inches for safe stowing of coins, jewel caches, and the rest of your small trinkets and valuables. To complete the deception, the Picture Safe is convincing enough at its ostensible job to fit inconspicuously on a desk or tabletop, while access to the hidden compartment is always just a slide away.

The sentimentality of desk-top family portraits would mar your rugged image? Don't despair; there's a solution for you, too. A companion covert tool is the Book Safe. It masquerades as an ordinary tome, but open its cover and it's not words you're looking at but 19 cubic inches of safe storage space for hiding goodies from prowling eyes and prying fingers.

Price: $8.99 for the Picture Safe; $7.50 for the Book Safe.

Supplier: Forever Safe.

Key Locker

The rendezvous is botched. Trudy the Tugboat was to meet you at the safe house on the dock at ten, toting the Cuban maritime pa-

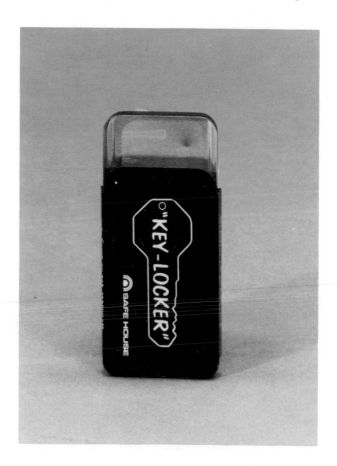

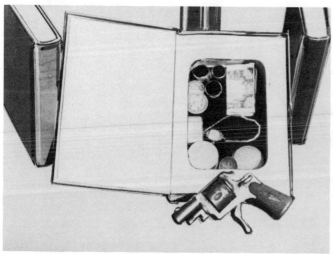

BOOK SAFE

pers she'd promised you. It's ten past ten and there's no Trudy. She has a knack for getting sidetracked with her pals at the Crawfish Inn. You know she'll arrive—eventually. But that's too late for you. You're due at HQ *now*. But you don't want Trudy, valuable papers in hand, roaming the docks all night. That's why you put the emergency plan into action.

You take the key that unlocks the front door, insert it into the Key-Locker, and with the attached magnet, clip all within the nearby drainpipe. Trudy will find it; this has happened before. She'll let herself in, put the booty under the floorboard, and let herself out again. You know she'll remember to put the key back in the Key-Locker because you buy her a six-pack every time she does.

Even if you don't have a rendezvous with Trudy, the Key-Locker is a handy item. Use this magnetic box to stash spare keys in all manner of metallic hiding places—under cars, inside gutters, beneath backyard barbeques. Key-Locker will snugly hold your spare keys and keep them removed from prying eyes but still accessible to you.

Price: $.69.

Supplier: Radio Shack.

Key Safe

The instructions were detailed and allowed for no improvisation. They had to be followed to the letter; that was made clear. Thus your bewilderment.

Carry no identification and no personal objects when you leave your home, the order specified. If you are caught, there must be nothing to link you with the service. So the labels were ripped out of your clothing; the billfold was left on the nightstand, and so were your keys.

The last was the rub. Fine and dandy to carry nothing that established who you were—but how were you to lock your home securely for the night and still manage to reenter it at mission's end?

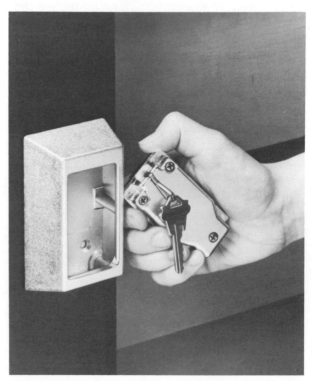

A brick through a window? A grand entrance indeed, but costly in repair bills—and potentially even costlier if an alert neighbor calls the police.

It is for quandaries such as this that the Key Safe exists. Mount it in an out-of-sight location or post it in plain sight, because even if a burglar discovers it, he will give up. Its rugged zinc-alloy construction and sturdy concealed screws will deter all but the most brutally persistent attempts at entry.

It can't be picked. Only the combination—which you program—will open it. At 4⅛ by 2½ by 2 inches deep, it offers room for several keys (or even a few microfilm rolls), and no matter what your mission, this cache will be there to welcome you home—and let you in.

Price: $19.95.

Supplier: Brookstone.

Magnetic Lock

The operation is in Iowa. But your brown thumb is no handicap, because the only crop you're harvesting is information. It's blooming everywhere, mainly because the Agency's bet is that *nobody* would ever think to look for stored secret documents in Iowa. That's why you've got computer tapes, microdots, even hard paper copies stowed in every cranny of your farm. The silo, chicken coop, garages, barns, main house, even the outhouse at the property's edge—all store priceless, sensitive facts about the nation's espionage operations.

Then the ominous word comes: The other side knows—all. And they've dispatched an old nemesis, the notorious Picklock Pete, to make hay with your crop.

Picklock is good, too. You know that. He'll elude the snarling dogs, circumvent the in-trusion alarms, sneak by the guards. He's done it before. But this time, you resolve, he will *not* do it.

So straightaway you lock up everything: every door, bulkhead, and access route. And you use the Magnetic Lock, because you know it will be Picklock's undoing.

That's because this waterproof, rust-resistant padlock is very difficult to break (the heavy chrome plating sees to that) and nearly impossible to pick. It responds only to a magnetic encoded key—the one in your possession—no others. *With* the key, opening the lock is a snap: The key is simply placed in a recess in the lock, a maneuver that can be accomplished with one hand and in the dark, even with gloves on. And it cleverly shuts

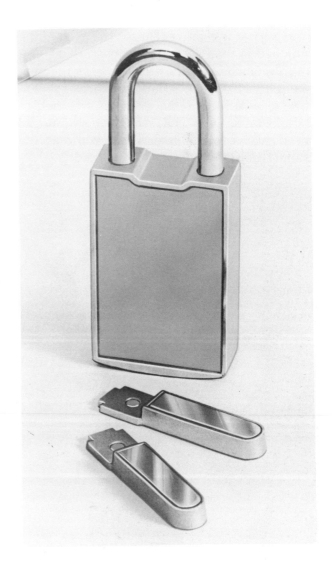

itself, too: Just rotate the shackle and, snap! it's locked.

At 3⅞ inches in length and with a shackle clearance of 1³⁄₁₆ inches, it's a versatile all-around lock, good not only for protecting precious papers but also for locking sea chests, bicycles . . . anything and anyplace a padlock would work.

Price: $8.95 (including two keys that open *only* your lock).

Supplier: Brookstone.

Security Door Lock

The courier is coming. That is the good news. The bad is that there's an impostor, one of a murderous breed, who's known to be in town, too. So you've been ordered to check credentials carefully, *without* exposing yourself to homicidal danger. That means you want and need access to the credentials while at the same time denying access to yourself.

Take a sigh of relief. It's possible. With the hundred-percent-steel Security Door Lock, you can have it all, safely.

This device works very much like a conventional chain lock, except better. A ring that fits over the door's knob attaches to a chain encased in steel tubing. The tube is connected to a 3-inch-long anchor bolt that goes into the door frame and is virtually impossible to rip out. It sounds complicated, but its use is simple. It's the misuse that's complicated, because the steel tubing *rolls* and wriggles if an intruder tries to file or saw through this Security Lock. And the ring can only be removed if the door is completely shut.

No courier is expected today? The Security Door Lock is still at your service as you inspect salesmen, delivery people, unfamiliar repairmen, and everybody else who shows up at your door. And you know that with the Security Door Lock, they will stay out *until* you decide to unhook this device.

Price: $7.95.

Supplier: Brookstone.

Wide-Angle Door Viewer

It's a top-secret conference in a safe apartment. But maybe, with its reinforced solid-steel door, the apartment is too safe. That's because all the Agency heavyweights are attending, and it's imperative that this conference be kept secret. That means no attention can be drawn to the meeting place. So there's no posting of guards outside the door, and no way of keeping track of whether it's friend or foe who comes knocking at the door.

All the Agency needs is to open the door and find a snooping reporter or a man from the other side. The disaster would be complete.

But there is no reason to suffer the luck of the draw when opening a door. Just install a Wide-Angle Door Viewer and you'll see all that's outside. Installation is simple, too: Drill a single hole and the job is done. Then you'll be treated to a wider angle of view (180 degrees) than any other peephole device on the market, promises the supplier.

Made of solid brass, it's not undecorative. And the Door Viewer fits all doors from 1³/₈ inches to 2¹/₈ inches in thickness.

Price: $9.95.

Supplier: Brookstone.

Money Belt

Dennis the Dip is the quarry, and Port Authority, the bustling Manhattan bus terminal, the battleground. "Just follow Dennis," the boss instructed—but the small smirk on his face told you there was more to this job

than that. And it hit you when you stopped at the cashier for a cash expense-account advance.

Dennis the Dip indeed. That was the ploy. Certainly Dennis was suspected of trucking with the other side—his dossier made clear that Dennis was a steady trafficker in purloined papers. No matter where the mark carried the papers, if they were on his body, Dennis's slick digits could be counted on to lift them; he was that good a pickpocket.

So that was the scam. A setup. You were being primed for the "rif," the reduction in force, another casualty of tightening budgets. Yes, while you were watching Dennis, he'd be watching you, and soon enough he would be sure to separate you from your wallet—money, ID, and all. Sure disgrace would follow.

Whew; you breathe a relieved sigh. Off comes the black cowhide belt. A tug on the hidden zipper, and the foot-long money compartment opens wide. The laugh is on Dennis. Let him pick your pockets. Everything of value now is securely stowed in your belt,

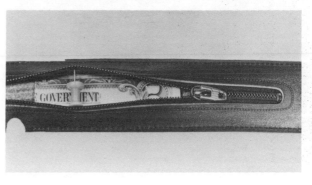

and no dip is agile enough to slip that off a mark.

Never would a pickpocket suspect that this belt is anything other than conventional. It's made of fashionable, supple cowhide in black or brown, and only the inside zippered compartment is distinctive. But that is enough to foil pickpockets—and keep you *off* the mark.

Price: $15.25 (available in even sizes, 34–42 inches).

Supplier: Brookstone.

NIGHT WATCH BOLT ALARM

Night Watch Bolt Alarm

You're taking the night off, and it's about time. You relax in the Jacuzzi; the water jets pulse and the wine flows. Intruders are the last thing you want to deal with. And the furthest thing from your mind.

But slipshod you're not. Polaroid's Night Watch Bolt Alarm is on the job. It's a combination device for double the security. A tough carbon-steel bolt slides into the door frame for extra locking power. And if a would-be intruder exerts the slightest pressure on the door, the built-in alarm lets loose with an angry, protesting howl—a noise loud enough to alert you and, in the process, probably scare off that intruder.

Suitable for nearly all doors, Night Watch Bolt Alarm is easily installed and just as easy to operate. It gets up to a full year of power on a single Polaroid Polapulse battery for long-term security.

Price: $14.95 (includes one battery; replacement batteries are $2.75 each).

Supplier: Markline.

Barricade Door Lock

There is insistently loud knocking at the door, and it's not the big bad wolf who has come calling. It is worse than that, and you know it. But you're still calm and unafraid even as the banging and thumping intensify. Because you know your door is totally barricaded against intruders.

That's the peace of mind delivered by the Barricade Door Lock. A clever device, it's crafted of durable metal and designed to block *all* door movement when it's in place. Pickproof, of course, and easily installed with just a few screws, the Barricade Door Lock will also give way at your touch of the one-finger release in the event an emergency inside (a fire, for instance) is driving you out.

Price: $9.95.

Supplier: Radio Shack.

Night Sentry

You're going to Beirut, and the travel orders came fast—too abruptly for you to make arrangements to move reams of confidential papers, caches of diamonds, and piles of top-secret gadgets from your house. But your unlived-in home will be a magnet for thieves. By the second night, when there are still no signs of life, every burglar in town will be partying in your livingroom. When you return, it will be to a stripped-bare dwelling.

Not, however, if Night Sentry is on the job. It replaces existing electrical wall switches (an installation that takes five minutes), and it's used exactly like a standard switch. Except Night Sentry comes with a memory. Program it to turn lights on and off at the intervals you command; or simply leave it alone and use it without the memory feature. Within twenty-four hours Night Sentry will have your routine down pat. Day after day your normal usage pattern will be automatically repeated, with slight variations to further baffle the plotting of would-be intruders, for as long as you're away.

Price: $29.95.

Supplier: Mountain West.

Warning Decals

You've been relocated to Venice, California, to the center of what's left of the entire world's hippy population. You're to blend in with the natives. The flea-bitten cottage they've stuck you in is perfect in terms of camouflage but woefully lacking in terms of security. Since you're supposed to be a penniless sandal maker, you've been living with nothing but the clothes on your back, a few bucks in your pocket, and a heap of purloined papers your partner is picking up next week. You must safeguard them in your cottage for the meantime, but you can't stay away from the sandal shop the whole week, and you don't have the cash for anything elaborate.

The situation is not enviable, but it's not terminal, either. Just take a few of your meager pennies and buy a pack of Radio Shack decals—"WARNING/Protected by a/ Radio Shack/Security System," they boldly proclaim. Mount them on doors and windows, and odds are that the warning alone will frighten off at least a few thieves, even if you have no security system to back up the threat.

Price: $.99 (for five).

Supplier: Radio Shack.

Tantalum Engraver

It's a small nuisance, but not one you can ignore: Whenever an assignment takes you into the field, you can count on returning to a barren office. Ashtrays, coffee mugs, even staplers—all are filched by co-workers, and so you must devote a day or more scurrying about in search of replacements whenever you return.

This rugged tantalum carbide-tip engraver will put an end to that. It will engrave initials—anything—into everything except diamonds. Marking depth is adjustable, too, for safe use on more delicate items like crystal wine glasses. And it's as easy to use as a pencil.

But office thieves are not the only ones who will be deterred. Take the engraver home and busy yourself writing identifying numbers on everything you own; burglars and robbers look askance at anything that bears such markings. Engrave a Social Security number, a driver's license number, anything that's unique. It's a cheap but effective way of sending criminals away empty-handed.

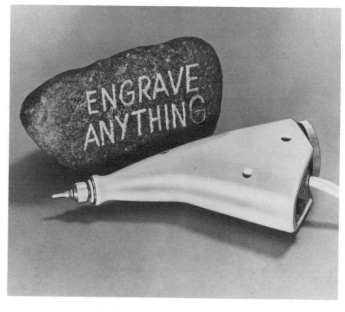

Price: $21.95 (a spare tantalum carbide tip costs $2.50; an optional diamond tip costs $11.25).

Supplier: Brookstone.

Rexell Shredders

Paper has always been a problem. Put a fact on paper and it is a record that makes it potentially dangerous. Ask Henry Kissinger, whose garbage cans at his Georgetown home have been combed routinely by journalists and agents alike. Just one top-secret note, a single confidential scrap of paper—that's all it would take to make wading through a mountain of fetid lasagna worthwhile. Dump ashes, coffee cups, discarded bits of lunch in your office trash can—it won't matter. The same is true at home. If a determined professional—or a just plain nosy person—believes what you throw out is valuable, he will gladly hold his nose with one hand and poke through the piles of rubbish with the other. He will do this, that is, unless you dramatize the pointlessness of the quest.

Rexell Shredders provide three acts and more of drama and a range of styles and security cuts to meet all needs. Your aim is simply to make piecing together your papers a nuisance? A low-priced Rexell fills the bill. Top-secret documents are involved and they must be thoroughly destroyed? Another Rexell can handle that.

The Ambassador RS-400, for instance, is a handsome piece of office furniture with a stylish teak finish and discreet black top. Feed it paper and it rapidly chews whole sheets into 3/16-inch shreds. Dual purposes are served by the Diplomat, too. It's a waste basket and a shredder, too. A Rexell unit perches directly above a conventional waste basket to make your circular filing all the more complete. The Verishred RS-9, on the other hand, is a strictly single minded machine with a voracious appetite. Cram it with papers as fast as you can; don't even bother to remove staples and paper clips. The Verishred won't mind. Instead it grinds it all into minute 1/32-inch shreds, and those are cuts that meet Department of Defense security standards. The same goes for Cross-Cut RS-9-CC, except it is even more committed to its destruction of paper. Not only are the shreds tiny, but Cross-Cut does as its name implies: Papers are cut and cut again to make all attempts at reassembly pointless. Cross-Cut even operates during power failures, via a manual control feature, and that is a key reason why it's the most widely used shredder in embassies and government offices around the world.

So put the office snoops out of business. Requisition a Rexell and—*whoosh*—your papers will be no more.

Prices: Ambassador—$845.
Diplomat Wastebasket—$595.
Verishred RS-9-1/32—$1595.
Cross Cut RS-9-CC—$2495.
(Other shredders are available from $650–$6995.)

Supplier: Rexell Shredders.

Auto Immobilizer

Princess Tuffi El-Joyride is your ward for the weekend, and you know she'll run you ragged. The princess, rambunctious to the core, is adept at the quick escape. Hers is an uncanny knack for disappearance, regardless of the hour, and it often is days before she turns up at a remote disco, casino, or yacht club.

That cannot happen this weekend. The mandate was firm. Just as inflexible, however, was the instruction that the princess is to be accorded utmost diplomatic cordiality. She must be treated with thoroughgoing respect—which rules out locking her in a closet for the duration.

There is a solution, however. Princess Tuffi has a passion for Professor Toru Tonaka and his particular brand of Sumo wrestling. Just bring him in for an exhibition and make a quick escape yourself. Slip down to the garage, enter her car, and in seconds—that's

all it takes—wire an Auto Immobilizer into place. Then let the princess sneak down to her car. It will start as always, but within eight seconds it will enigmatically stall. And it will not start again. The problem is not to be found under the hood. That's because the Auto Immobilizer, the cause of this "malfunction," is stowed under the dashboard.

When it's time to release the princess, just pay a return visit to her vehicle. Switch the Immobilizer to Off and the car will function normally—with no one the wiser if the Auto Immobilizer is left in place. Because there is no telling when this weekend's success will prompt an encore order to watch over the slippery highness once again.

In the time it takes to read this report, a professional car thief can enter your car, start it, and zoom away. Thirty seconds is how long the job takes. But that is also about how long it takes to install an Auto Immobilizer. Just attach two wires and the job is done. Small ($2\frac{1}{2}'' \times 2'' \times 1\frac{5}{8}''$) and easily hidden under a seat or dashboard, the Auto Immobilizer safely and securely paralyzes a car's ignition system—and that is enough to deter all but the most skilled and persistent thieves.

Sorry, but diesel cars are out of luck. The Immobilizer functions only on gasoline-powered models.

Price: $34.95.

Supplier: Brookstone.

The Ankler

You're chasing the suspect down a Parisian *rue*. Your legs pump furiously; your breath is coming harder. Then you stumble, trip over a discarded rind of brie . . . and the roll of enemy microfilm that was in your shirt pocket is disgorged. It flies out and tumbles into the Seine. A disgrace! The mission is in ruins.

Inventory the loss: the suspect; microfilm; a Cross pen set; a Zippo. All gone forever. It is time to resolve that that will never happen again. And it needn't be an idle oath. The Ankler is made to prevent such mishaps.

The Ankler is a second sock, *sans* feet but *with* convenient built-in pouches for covert and secure stowing of valuables. Money, combs, pens, even microfilm and small knives are regular fare for the Ankler's pockets. Slide the nylon-web Ankler on, shove your tools within, and now you are *really* ready for fast romps and the occasional faster fall.

You're prepared for casual frisks as well. (Many stop before inspecting the ankles.) And, if the spirit strikes, a rapid game of basketball or a strenuous mountain climb. No matter the arduous circumstances, the Ankler is designed to hold your belongings out of view but firmly in place. The construction of the Ankler makes it comfortable, and its synthetic fabric allows for "breathing," so there is scant sweat buildup. One size fits all.

Price: $9.

Supplier: Ankler Designs.

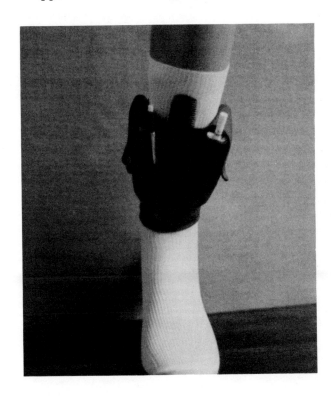

STAYING ALIVE: PERSONAL PROTECTION

THERE'S A WAR GOING ON, *and it's not limited to the pages of adventure novels and spy thrillers. In the 1950s KGB killer Bogdan Stashinskiy employed an ingenious "gas gun" (which left its victims to die a death resembling a heart attack) to slay dozens of Eastern European anti-Communists. In the 1970s in England, dozens more Eastern Europeans died as a result of KGB poison darts. How many victims have there been—of this side's killers . . . of that side's? Nobody knows. Nobody will venture a guess. Hundreds? Thousands, more probably.*

Spies are not the only fatalities. Another kind of war—one every bit as deadly—is now sweeping this nation's cities, small towns, and suburbs. The body count is also rising. A recent year tallied 21,500 murders nationwide; 76,000 reported rapes; 467,000 robberies; 614,000 instances of aggravated assault.

The facts are ugly, but an ugly response is not the only possibility. Not with The Complete Spy's *self-protection gear for spies and civilians alike.*

Politeness, mind you, is not the only rationale for gentleness. Law enforcement officials, for instance, incline to look askance—and worse—when the citizenry takes to blasting one another with cannons. Reasonable force is the only permissible response by a civilian to an attack, although what constitutes reasonable force is a debate that can fill pages . . . and grueling hours of courtroom time. Use the defensive gear presented here and you'll be likely to avoid all that.

Avoidance of legal rigamarole is not the only advantage of defensive equipment. It can preserve your pacifistic ideals, as well as your very being.

Multi-Strike

This is a foe you want to put down but not out, at least not permanently. Multi-Strike is the solutions—and the plural is intentional.

A semiautomatic air pistol, Multi-Strike readily accommodates different ammunition rounds for different purposes. The threat is severe and imminent? Hit the enemy with a Tear Gas round and you'll drive him to tears, but without lasting consequences. It's a mission where you need a loud diversion? Detonate a few Cracker rounds and you'll saturate the area with resonating noise and confusing sounds. Just who is this antagonist? Find out for sure, but at your convenience. Load Multi-Strike with the Dye Marker and you'll thoroughly coat any assailant with vivid, indelible color—and his identity will be indisputable.
Load types are quickly changed as necessary, and for added certainty and convenience, Multi-Strike's ammo is packed in three-round magazines. Effective range is approximately 100 feet.

Prices: Multi-Strike—$280.
Tear Gas Load—$30.
Dye Marker—$30.
Cracker—$30.

Supplier: LEA.

Search Alert

You're sure he's carrying a weapon—a gun, or at least a knife. But a frisk turns up nothing. Should you trust him? Not yet. First subject him to a probe with Search Alert, an electronic frisker (just like the ones in use in airports worldwide) that shrilly reacts to the presence of metal. Physical contact with the subject is not necessary (let him howl about privacy rights all he wants; you're violating none of them with Search Alert), yet no matter where a weapon is concealed—even in cleverly unorthodox spots like the anal cavity—Search Alert will detect it.

Battery-operated and lightweight (1 pound) for portability, Search Alert features adjustable sensitivity to screen out false alarms caused by coins and keys and screen in real, dangerous alarms caused by weapons. A pouch and wrist strap are also included.

Price: $150.

Supplier: LEA.

Bulletproof Vest

You open the door.

Viktor's gold tooth shines back at you.

The Hungarian killer is smiling. That is bad news. He never expresses good humor except when his mark is in his sight.

Homicide is Viktor's joke, and you are to be the butt of his macabre humor.

The long-barrel .357-magnum pistol crackles. The roar is deafening. The bullet smashes the sound barrier and it aims directly at your heart at a rib-fragmenting speed of 1400 feet per second.

But the laugh is on Viktor.

Pop! It's at this moment that "RIP" is supposed to be written on your tombstone. But that inscription is premature. The .357 slug harmlessly bounces into the distance. You are wearing your Matthews bulletproof vest.

Soft-style body armor made of Kevlar—the comfortable, flexible, lightweight material recommended by the National Institute of Law Enforcement and Criminal Justice—the Matthews vests have undergone official testing by the US Department of the Army.

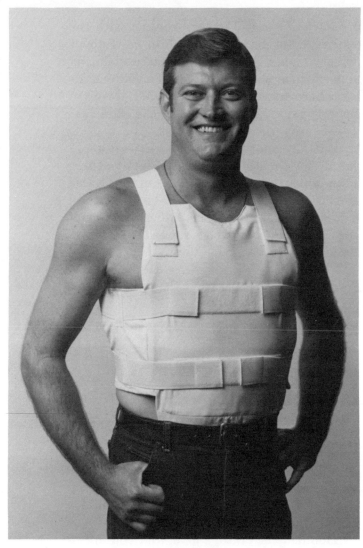

The verdict? "There were no penetrations of the samples," judged the program manager of the army's Lightweight Armor Program. Appropriate as that dryly unenthusiastic language is for reporting experimental results, jubilation is what you'll express if you are wearing a Matthews vest and there's "no penetration" after a hired killer or a demented drooler of an assassin takes a shot at your heart.

That is precisely what the Matthews vest is designed to deliver: safety even when the wearer is subjected to point-blank gunfire. Not only does the bulletproof vest stop the speeding projectile, but there will be no "blunt trauma," that is, no painful bruises or cracked rips due to the shattering force of the bullet's impact. Because the Matthews vest absorbs all that abuse uncomplainingly.

Don a Model K-10, for instance, and that 2-pound vest shields against most common handguns (such as .22-, .32-. .38-, and .45-caliber pistols). Model K-16 is a step up in protection. At 2¾ pounds, it repels all that its little brother chases off plus .357 magnum and "00" buck from a shotgun. Model K-22 (3½ pounds) does all that and also snears at huge .41- and .44-magnum slugs.

You're right: Elephant guns and bazookas will still kill you. But little else will. That's why the Matthews vest and similar garb are fast becoming *de rigueur* for police, heads of state, and even the most dapper spies.

Prices: Model K-10—$120.
Model K-16—$150.
Model K-22—$180.

(Detachable side panels, for still greater protection, add $25.00, $27.50, and $30.00, respectively, to the cost.)

Supplier: Matthews Police Supply Company.

Card Case Armor

The best defense may be a good offense—but this uniquely potent card case armor pad does double duty. Slide these tempered steel plates into your business card or credential case and you've immediately transformed it into a tiny bulletproof shield, one designed to afford limited-area ballistic protection against most handgun calibers. Stow the case in a breast pocket that covers your heart, say, and at least that delicate zone is shielded. That's the defensive component.

The offense may be better still. The steel plates are finely sharpened on three edges, and with the plates in place in your card case, you've got a disguised *shuriken,* an Oriental hybrid of the knife and dart and a deadly weapon in any arsenal. Just heave

the case hard at a foe's neck and he's an adversary who is sure to be distracted, if not neutralized.

Two hardened and honed plates come in each set, and they fit comfortably within a standard business card case. Or within a 3-by-5-inch federal ID–size case.

Price: $20
(specify either 2″ × 3.5″ or 3″ × 5″ when ordering).

Supplier: ASP.

Attaché Armor Pad

The heavy gun crackles. You don't look because you know the bullet is heading straight your way. The fatal slug smacks into you with a sickening thud—but it bounces away miraculously and you're unharmed, ready to retaliate. No, you're not *Superman* and that was no miracle . . . except one made by science.

An instant fit in most attaché cases, this

briefcase armor pad affords nine thick layers of Kevlar protection packed into a not-inelegant black nylon pouch. That's ample armor to ward off most handgun bullets. Better still, if the corporate pose is not your guise, the attaché case can be dispensed with: The nylon case accommodatingly fits under clothing for more immediate and intimate protection. So, whether your cover is that of a businessman or a taxi driver, a waitress or musician, this lightweight armor pad provides reliable protection against most caliber bullets.

Price: $100.

Supplier: ASP.

Powerhorn

There are times—very bad ones—when there's no option left except to shout, scream, bellow for help . . . and just hope somebody hears you. Powerhorn, a pocket-size howler, does that work for you and it does it better.

Whenever a mugger—or worse—enters your range, just let Powerhorn rip. The noise is loud enough to scare away most intruders, and in the bargain, it will be heard up to a half-mile away.

Price: $5.95.

Supplier: Radio Shack.

Constable's Whistle

You're on a stakeout in front of Grand Central Station. Your mission is to blend into the crowd but still be able and ready to signal your team when Hawkeyed Hannah darts past the kiosk. But the signal has to be a subtle one; if Hannah sees it, she'll fly the coop.

So just give a toot on your authentic Constable's Whistle. Hannah will think nothing of it. In her book you'll be just another Limey tourist or a doorman hailing a cab. Yet your whistle will make sufficient noise to alert the troops—indeed, it's noisy enough to awaken a camp full of Cub Scouts. Plus you might might get a cab in the bargain.

That's because this whistle is identical to the authoritative ones used by London's bobbies for over a century. Made of polished nickel-plated brass, it sounds a shrill, two-tone whistle—and each whistle is tested for authenticity of tone.

Once Hannah is safely bagged, remember to keep this small (3¼″ long) and lightweight (1.3 ounce) whistle handy. It's good for calling the dog, scaring off prowlers, and summoning help. Plus it's designed to be worn around the neck, where it's decorative as well as secure.

Price: $6.50.

Supplier: Brookstone.

Commando Watchband

Timing on this night's mission is critical. The work is delicate, dangerous. Your combined strike must come at precisely the right moment, so you and your comrades have synchronized your watches. But the damn glow! The illumination from your timepieces mocks the care and stealth of your operation. Maybe your target cannot tell time from your watch, but as you near his lair, he will surely be able to tell you're coming. The insistent glare of the watches ensures that.

That's right: Many watches glow in the night. And many operations have been blown as a result. But not if the participants sheath their timepieces in Commando Watchbands, because this resin-treated nylon web watchband features a crystal-covering strap for concealment and also for protection of the watch face.

Rot resistant, wearable underwater, and washable, the Commando Watchband quickly replaces most regular bands and adapts to nearly all watches. And the Velcro Hook-n-Loop closure snaps securely over most crystals.

Available in an assortment of colors (olive drab, black, navy, sage green, and red), the sizes range from 6¾ inches through 8½ inches (in ¼-inch increments). Other sizes are available at extra cost.

Price: $5.50.

Supplier: Brigade Quartermasters.

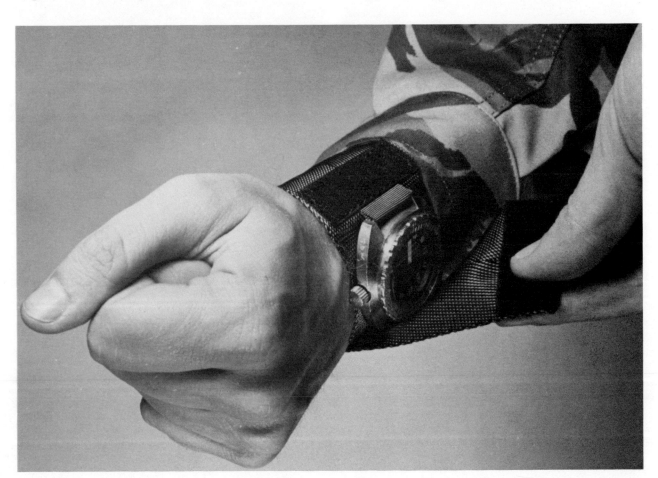

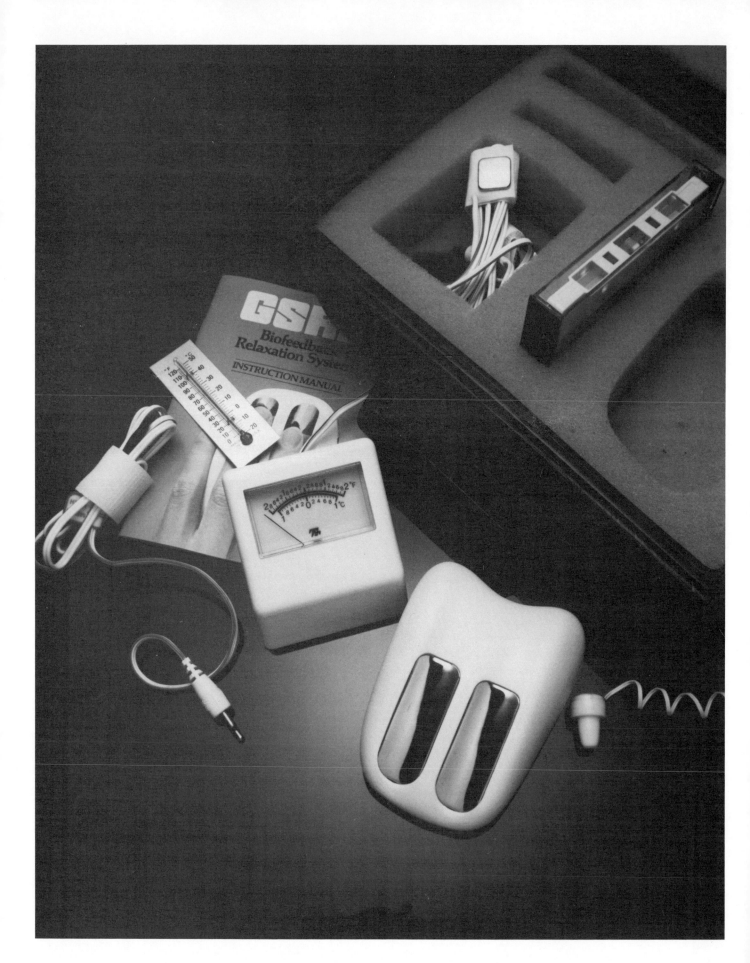

GSR 2 Biofeedback Monitor

You've been sent to East Germany precisely to be caught and questioned as a spy. And you'd better be calm as a manikin—or you'll wind up stiffer than one. You know you must have utter mastery over your reactions to stress. So you'll learn how with a GSR 2.

Palm-size, the GSR 2 converts tension-related changes in your skin-pore size into sound; the higher the pitch, the higher the level of stress. To test stress levels, just rest two fingers on the sensory plates and absorb the relaxation suggestions offered on the cassette tape that accompanies GSR 2—or simply follow the written instructions that are also included—and within seconds the monitor's pitch will lower, because your stress level is already dropping.

The more you use GSR 2, the lower your stress level will drop and the faster it will do so. Quickly enough you'll be relaxing without the machine in tow—and that means, no matter how stressful a situation, you'll be in complete control and all the more able to respond, because you're now in charge of your tension.

Not only spies on deeply covert missions benefit from GSR 2. Think of the tension that coursed through your body when you last argued with a boss or lover. GSR 2, the supplier says, will improve all performances. And the US Olympic Nordic Ski team uses these units when in training.

For even more thorough monitoring, an optional package (GSR/TEMP 2) ups GSR 2's capabilities to include temperature measurement—an important stress indicator—and adds a meter so the subject can see as well as hear his progress toward stress control. Two remote sensors round out these options and allow for measurement of stress with your hands free.

Price: $49 ($99 for GSR/TEMP 2).

Supplier: Sharper Image.

ANTIPERSONNEL WARFARE: THE TOOLS OF DOING OTHERS IN

JAMES BOND DOTES ON GUNS. *At first he favored a temperamental .32 Beretta, but MI-6's armorer cajoled 007 to pick a more consistently reliable gun, and eventually Bond adopted a Walther PPK. But 007 is the exception in the espionage world. Guns may kill people . . . but guns are not the only tools to this end, and that's a fact clever spies know well.*

Just take a glance at the armaments concocted by the CIA's Technical Services Division during the agency's quarrel with Fidel Castro. In the first stage of this undeclared war, the CIA was piqued but not homicidal. It contented itself with devising annoyances to harass the Cuban, including a plot to dust his shoes with thallium salts, a depilatory potent enough to cause the Bearded One's facial and body hair to fall out in tufts. When all stunts of that Puckish sort flopped, the CIA turned nasty and spun out successive scenarios to: treat Castro's cigars with botulism; rig an attractively rare seashell with a bomb and conspicuously deposit this death trap in one of Castro's favorite diving spots; and in a further upping of the ante, contaminate Castro's wet suit with a disease-causing fungus and saturate his diving respirator with tuberculosis-causing germs.

None of that exotica finds its way into The Complete Spy*—which is well, since none of it worked; Castro laughed at the CIA through its every move and laughed all the harder when these bizarrely madcap methods were revealed in testimony before public sessions of the US Congress.*

But plenty of exotica are featured in the following pages, including concealed blowguns, metal knuckles, weighted gloves, disguised knives, and a cornucopia of more straightforwardly lethal and near-lethal weaponry. Is all this gear legal? To the best of our knowledge, yes. But again we stress: check with local authorities before buying any *weaponry. That stitch in time can save nine years or more in jail.*

Thompson Submachine Gun

It was born in the fecund military mind of Brigadier General John T. Thompson and bred out of the US Army's infelicitous experiences in trench combat during that Great War. A trench broom, Thompson euphemistically called his lightweight, rapid-firing invention. "Tommy gun," is what everybody else said.

This was a brilliant martial innovation, but Thompson nonetheless lived to regret his handiwork. Because it was developed too late (1920) to be put into wartime service, the military passed on purchasing the general's gun. Law enforcement agencies, too, regarded the weapon with skepticism, in the main because they feared its spray of bullets would endanger bystanders.

None of that dampened the underworld's interest, and through a curious loophole in most firearms possession laws of the 1920's—regulations that aimed to prevent carrying *concealed* weapons—it was perfectly legal to carry publicly a Thompson. So the mob freely, brazenly, and murderously took to displaying and using the Tommy gun in that roaring Prohibition decade. Prices skyrocketed to $175 for a standard model in the legal marketplace; and following the imposition of restrictions in many localities, prices hit higher than $2000 as the gun gained increasing popularity and notoriety. And for many years the Tommy gun continued to command those steep tariffs, since it quite simply was the best weapon for many of the "wettest" jobs.

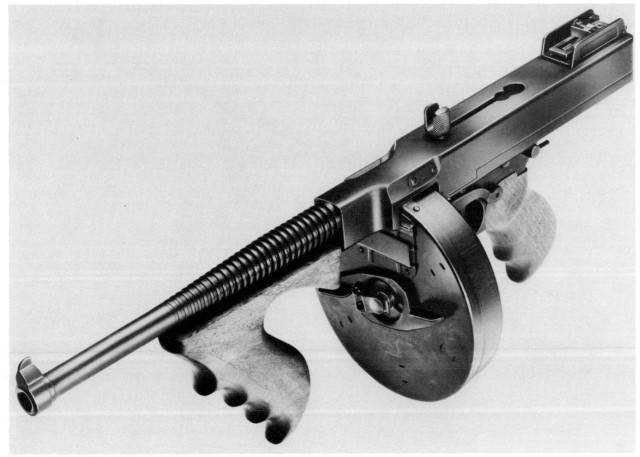

STANDARD TOMMY GUN

DRUM MAGAZINE

That's all history now. Far better and faster-shooting automatics are commonplace. But the lure and lore of the Tommy gun remains potent—powerful enough, in fact, so that the original manufacturer still puts out an array of Tommy guns . . . for collectors, buffs, and spies and others with every weapon in their personal arsenals.

Understand, this is not the Thompson of old. Or rather, it is an exact copy—with a critical difference. The new Thompson is a semiautomatic; the trigger must be pulled for every shot. No more *sput-sput-sput* of incessantly streaming bullets. But the rest of the machine gun is unchanged, and that is why it's a must for many.

Cost is no obstacle. Factor in inflation and these weapons are far cheaper now; and the range of choices remains wide. There's the full-length standard model, a menacing .45-

THOMPSON PISTOL

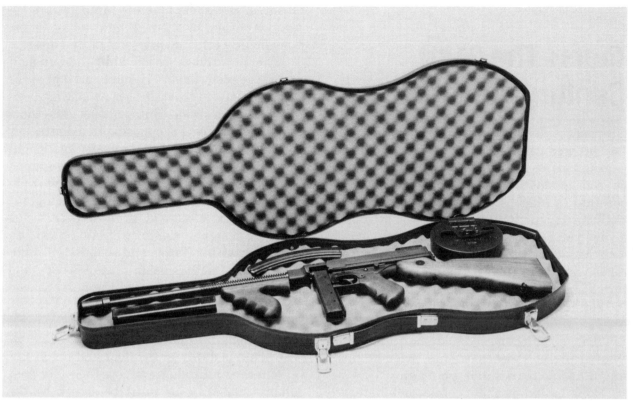

VIOLIN CASE

caliber boomer of a gun with a stock 20-shot magazine; a shorter, lighter, pistol-length .45 Thompson that comes with a 30-round clip; and an optional 39-shot drum magazine for even more ready firepower.

Tote a Thompson in the field and, granted, you are outgunned. The opposition will come armed with state-of-the-art guns like Uzi, MAC, and H & K submachine guns and pistols—diminutive, featherweight machines with bottomless bullet clips and a remorseless willingness to shoot still more. But maybe you've an edge nonetheless. Because with the Thompson you have reams of history on your side. And an incalculable shock value—especially if you extract your Tommy from an authentic, old-fashioned violin case. Nobody will believe it. Until you open fire.

Prices: Standard Tommy Gun—$469.95.
Thompson Pistol—$469.95.
Drum Magazine—$69.95.
Violin Case—$74.50.

Supplier: Auto-Ordnance Corp. (Note: A Federal Firearms License is required for mail-order purchase of guns. Write Auto-Ordnance for the name of a local distributor, from whom the guns can be bought legally and without special permits.)

Taser: The 21st Century Weapon

The bruiser pants as he eyes you. The gargantuan brute is actually salivating at what for him is the tasty prospect of pulverizing you into so much dog food. This, for you, is, shall we say, unappetizing. But you've made a vow, you recall. It's on the back bumper of your car—I Brake For Animals, the sticker reads, and you take seriously the biblical commandment not to take a life.

You shiver as the maniac closes in. You almost wish that animals—and others—could fend for themselves, damnit, because this is one of those moments when it just might be fine to own and use a gun.

Hold on—what about comic-book heroes? They don't resort to firearms. Not Batman, Wonder Woman, or even the Hulk. But that's kid stuff, the fiction of the young, you object.

Granted. But some juvenile fantasies are reality. And one of them is here today to get you—neatly and cleanly—out of this mess.

The Taser does the job while answering a pacifist's every wish. It hurts no one—not permanently, at least. It does no lasting damage to human tissue. But it nonetheless thoroughly transforms the most spirited attacker into a whining pile of protoplasm, and it will accomplish this white magic in seconds. That's because the Taser works on the principle that the body's nervous system is a giant and complex electrical grid—one that the Taser is designed to short circuit. Shoot an assailant with a Taser, and its burst of high-voltage electricity smashes into his body and assumes vigorous control of the nervous system. Pain is instantaneous (but short-lived), and so is an immobilizing series of muscle contractions, twitches, and spasms. *Bamm!* The brute is down on the floor and helpless.

There is a catch, however. To render that enemy into pulp, he must be struck by the Taser's tiny darts. Those barbed contacts are the medium through which the Taser's juice flows (alas, it is only in comics that all this happens in thin air). So a bit of aiming is required. But strike the foe with the darts, and for as long as the Taser's trigger is pulled, decapacitating electricity will flow into his body. In most cases, enough power is transmitted so that even after the trigger is released, the assailant will remain down and out for many more minutes—and yes, the Taser's power easily carries through clothes.

Of course, the Taser is fully portable. Weight is just 1½ pounds and length is 9 inches, so ready concealment is possible. But the design is close kin to a flashlight (one is even built in), and that makes for an effectively innocuous disguise.

So far that's all good news. There is a touch of bad. Because the Taser is comparable to a .38-caliber revolver in stopping power, a firearms permit is required for possession in some localities. But fill out the papers and, with a Taser in hand, thou shall not kill—yet thou shall not suffer pains or fears, either.

Price: $279.95 (options and more elaborate configurations can push the price to $400.00 and higher).

Supplier: Quality Creations.

Security Blanket

You *could* cuddle up with this blanket at night—but not for warmth. Security and freedom from assailants, not heat, are what the Security Blanket provides. Conjure up this unpleasant image: a gorilla, the three-hundred-pound variety with tattoo-emblazoned arms as large as your thighs, is about to crush you into very small and hugely painful particles. You have no taste for guns—or maybe your community imposes strict and prohibitive regulations regarding packing firearms in public—so that explosive option is out. But that does not leave you at this ape's untender mercy.

A light bulb flashes—but if it is the Security Blanket's bulb that does the flashing, that will be that for the threat your would-be mauler poses. While it looks like a run-of-the-mill flashlight, the Security Blanket shoots out a beam of light consisting of six million lumens, which is 25,000 times brighter than the light of a conventional bulb. Harmless as a light bulb sounds, the Security Blanket's potent flash stuns the eyes of any attacker and leaves him temporarily blinded and thrashing around in the darkness. Several minutes will pass before he regains his vision (and *no* permanent harm is inflicted). That's time aplenty for you to scurry to safety or to turn the tables and physically incapacitate the rotter.

Fully portable—the Security Blanket operates on 9-volt batteries—this potent but nonlethal weapon's secret is in the sophisticated, ultrahigh-intensity bulbs that concentrate maximum energy in a single, abruptly short burst. One flash per bulb is all you get,

however, and spare bulbs cost six dollars apiece.

Price: $110.

Supplier: Communications Control Systems.

Aluminum Knuckles

Look at a street fighter's hands when next you're in a corner saloon. Sidle up—be courteous, mind you—and take a strong, long peek. What you will see is a gnarled mess of bone and skin. Every bare-fisted punch into bone takes a toll—in scraped skin and painful, broken knuckles.

But that is the direct, simple way of dealing with foes. In espionage work few things are simple and absolutely nothing is direct. Especially not when technology offers improvements.

Like aluminum knuckles. Go ahead: Slide a pair on. And when next a sidewalk tough or an enemy from the other side taunts you, just smile. Then bash him one, or two or three times in the face. He *will* get your

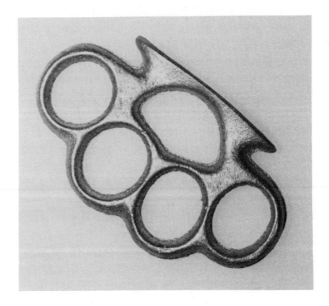

message—and hard it will be. But you will suffer no pain, no hurt hands for your strenuous efforts.

Of course, aluminum knuckles—a lightweight but just as strong version of the old-fashioned brass knuckles that once spiced fights in turn-of-the-century America—are not exactly legal. Law enforcement agents will frown on their use in a fight; indeed, at their possession. Which is why they are not sold or marketed as a fighting tool. No, aluminum knuckles are *paperweights*. Remember that: paperweights, for use as desk accessories. And, fact is, they would go very well on a desk top. Especially when the boss turns down a request for a raise . . . or a subordinate becomes exceptionally obstreperous.

Price: $6.

Supplier: ASP.

Heavy Hand

Thank god it's snowing, you smile to yourself while making your way down a bustling Berlin *Strasse*. As the flakes pile up on your trench coat, you reach into the pockets and don your gloves. Brrr, you mime as you cautiously survey the passersby. Nobody takes note.

You make the sharp right, as instructed, and deliberately pace deeper into the dark alley. It's still cold. You rub the palms of your gloved hands together. "Otto," you hiss. "Otto!"

Then you hear the creak of a heavy foot in the snow behind you.

"Otto is not late, *Mein Herr*. He is dead. There will be no exchange."

You wheel around to confront the speaker. Like a discus thrower, the force of the turn rushes up your body. And into your hands.

The gloved fist pounds into the man. He is

bigger than you; much bigger. With a square-jawed strength. But at the sharp contact of your fist, he gasps out a huge breath and abruptly drops to the ground. He has joined your informant, Otto, in death.

Yours is not the devastating punch of Sonny Liston or Jack Dempsey. Not ordinarily. But with the help of Heavy Hand, you become a slugger in any league. That's because Heavy Hand is not a conventional glove. Certainly it is made of soft but durable deerskin, and the appearance is normal. But every Heavy Hand comes with an extra feature: The knuckle and fist areas are padded and packed with lead shot, to make every punch count just a little bit more. Ouch! And ouch again. Because with Heavy Hand, every puncher is a world-class hitter.

Price: $50 (state size when ordering: S, M, L, XL).

Supplier: ASP.

Blowpen

You're trapped in an alley when you see him coming. His knife glistens in the macabre glimmer of the streetlight. It's the kill he's after, nothing less, and you are the target.

Forget the gun in your holster. The sound will alert everybody, friend and foe alike. That is why your foe is waving his blade. So you reach into your shirt pocket and pull out a pen.

"Writing your will?" The man cackles in a hot-breathed sneer.

Nope, you mutter under your breath. "It's *your* last testament, old chum."

You raise the pen to your lips and blow hard. The deadly dart shoots out and straight into your enemy. And you're the winner.

That's right—Blowpen is a blowgun, discreetly, surreptitiously disguised as a standard ball-point pen. A miniature version of the lethal weapon long used by South American Indians, this diminutive blowgun is designed for use in times and places where secrecy is a must or smallness is a necessity. Yet despite the reduced size, a puff from your lungs is all it takes to get the fast-flying darts out and doing their deadly jobs.

Price: $25 (a pack of five darts is included in the price; poison is not).

Supplier: ASP.

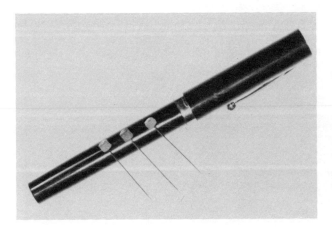

Weeping Eye

It is not you who will do the crying when you carry the Weeping Eye. No, you will do the victorious rejoicing. Your opponents will corner the market on unhappiness—the mortal variety.

This is the holster for times when weapon-concealment checks are anticipated and must be circumvented: crossing through Customs, meetings with opposition police agents—the Weeping Eye makes these encounters safe. Wear one and you needn't go "naked," because your weapon will escape all but the most thoroughgoing and intimate inspection. That's because with this unique holster, there's a built-in answer to the hoary Mae West question: "Is that a pistol in your pocket or are you glad to see me?"

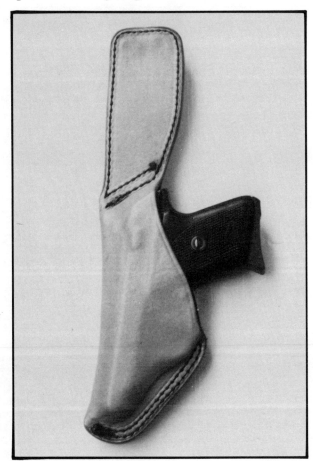

You are not glad. Hardly. But you are packing a pistol. Hidden in your groin area, the Weeping Eye securely holds your small-caliber gun until action calls. A fast flick of your zipper with your left hand, and whoosh, your right hand has your gun out and ready for furious firing. There's bad news for lefties, however: Due to the cut of men's trousers, the manufacturer reports that the Weeping Eye is not a practical holster for left-handed operatives. For them it's go weaponless—or become ambidextrous, which is the far better solution.

Do you doubt the Weeping Eye's immunity to detection? Then ask yourself this question: Would you want to fondle a stranger's crotch?

Price: $50.

Supplier: ASP.

Ankle Holster

"Excuse me, I've got an itch," you say off-handedly to your captor, and you bend down to scratch your ankle. Except the relief you seek has nothing to do with alleviating a skin irritation, because in a flash of your hand, you've capitalized on the other side's sloppy oversight—and your gun is out of its ankle holster and blasting away.

An ankle holster cannot be counted on to escape all frisks and pat-downs, but it will elude many. Besides, the ankle is always an inconspicuous—but still convenient—place to stow a handgun; a place that's in easy reach but definitely out of sight. And this extremely lightweight nylon Ankle Holster

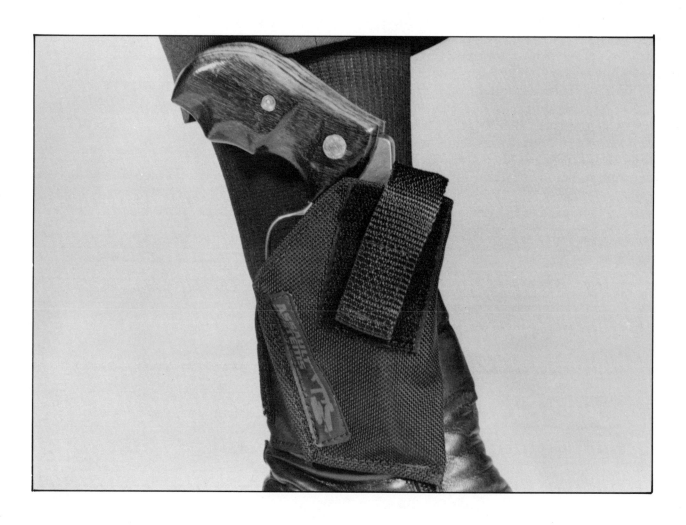

affords those benefits plus a confident comfort. For starters, the nylon is rugged 11-oz. Dupont Cordura, a fabric with the look of canvas but twice the strength. There's built-in rubber padding to shield the ankle bones from the gun's metal. And the nylon material breathes easily to minimize perspiration. But even so, you'll know your gun is always in place, since there's a high-strength Velcro fastener expressly designed to hold a gun in its holster reliably but still keep it ready for quick action.

Price: $30.

Supplier: Assault Systems.

Shoulder Holster

Go ahead, strut your stuff. Show them you mean business—and display your weaponry in a shoulder holster that's brazenly worn outside your shirt or jacket.

Made of ballistic nylon that's five layers thick, this Unconcealed Shoulder Holster is stronger than leather but lighter (just 8 ounces), and extremely comfortable because it speedily conforms to your body. All black and with black hardware, it also features a Velcro strap for securing your weapon in place.

Nylon sounds right for you. But your work is of a different, more covert sort, and only a Concealable Shoulder Rig will do?

CONCEALABLE RIG

UNCONCEALED SHOULDER HOLSTER

Don't try to hide this hulk of an unconcealed holster. Opt instead for its trimmer kin, a rig designed for inconspicuous reliability, all in black again, and with an elastic back strap that allows for free movement of both arms.

Prices: Unconcealed Shoulder Holster—$35.
Concealable Rig—$40.

Supplier: Assault Systems.

The Judge

The mission is a desperate one. Concealment is no longer necessary or desirable. You know they're coming after you; they know you're coming after them. Niceties are out. Seconds count at this deadly stage. Don't hide your gun; wear it. Keep it handy on a belt loop for ready use. But do that securely in the Judge.

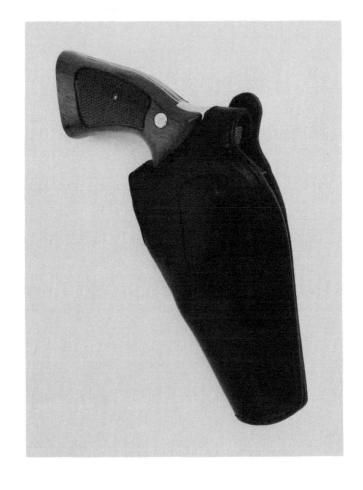

Standard-issue equipment of the Los Angeles Police Department and the California Highway Patrol not just because of the Judge's streamlined good looks, this high-performance holster is designed, foremost and uncompromisingly, to give the wearer the fastest draw around, safely. A unique built-in spring allows this by holding the holster firmly closed at all times—except for those few moments when you apply anxious pressure on the pistol butt, and in response the entire front of the holster spreads open to permit fast and free removal of the gun.

Made of saddle leather with a suede lining, the Judge is not just for street fights and quick-draw contests, however. It's an always handsome and reliable way to store a pistol, and because the case envelops the trigger, it's safe, too.

Price: $55.

Supplier: Bianchi Gunleather.

Sam Browne Belt

You will hear agents and soldiers say it just before they go off to war: "I've got Sam Browne on my side," as a contented look crosses their face. But Sam Browne is no comrade or spirit. It's a belt; one with a history.

British general Sir Samuel Browne, a nineteenth-century warrior in Her Majesty's service, was a man who stolidly kept a stiff upper lip and was simply not to be swayed from his martial duty. Even when he lost his left arm in combat, Browne persisted—although it took ingenuity to do it. Before, Browne, like other soldiers of his era, went into combat with his left hand supporting his sword in a state of steady preparedness. That he could no longer do, so to keep his sword in a safe, immobile position, Browne invented a

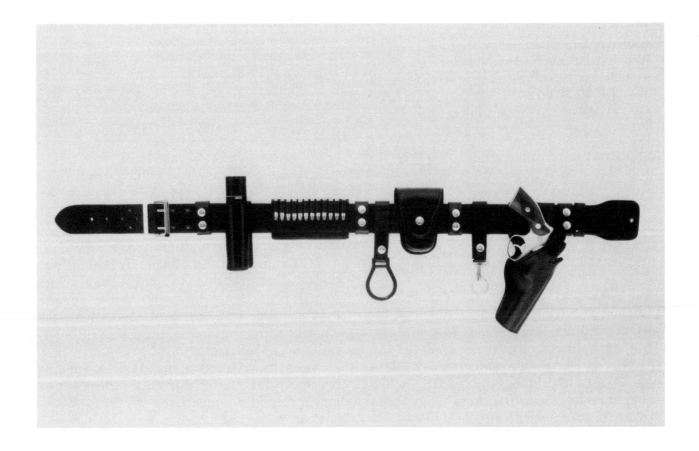

durable belt with a shoulderstrap to do the job of his lost left arm.

Nowadays the sword is largely forgotten and so is the safety strap that was the key to Browne's design. But his belt, both because of Browne's personal story and also since the belt itself proved to be rugged and strong, lives on. And it does so superbly in the 2¼-inch-wide Bianchi update of the traditional Sam Browne.

Can't imagine why a police officer, soldier, or spy with an especially dirty piece of fieldwork before him would require a special belt? Think again. The belt is the handiest place to hold many of the tools of the trade: guns, knives, handcuffs, tear gas, spare ammunition. Weight escalates fast, and a conventional belt would give way and shred under the strain. Not so a Sam Browne. It's built to carry pounds of gear reliably and to do it comfortably, even stylishly.

A suede lining for nonslip use is standard. Construction is of full leather, with a hand finish. Hardware is your choice of brass or chrome finish. Available in waist sizes 26 inches to 46 inches.

Price: $35.50. (Note: price as illustrated is $125.50. Breakdown is like this: Belt—$35.50; Holster—$44.00; Cuff Case—$15.00; Spare Cartridge Slide—$15.00; Mace/Teargas Holder—$12.50; Baton Ring—$3.50.)

Supplier: Bianchi Gunleather.

Bandolier

This is not your sort of work. Sipping Dom Perignon and deftly probing a diplomat for secrets of his statecraft is more to your taste. This assignment, however—though you shudder at the prospect—will require bullets. Dozens of them. And you're baffled about how best to carry them. Loose in a pocket? In your mouth?

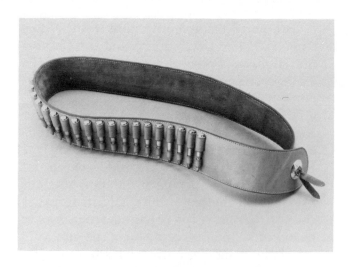

Nope. In the Bandolier. It's the convenient and stylish way to tote up to forty slugs wherever you go. Made of leather and with a suede lining, Bandolier measures 3½ inches wide and 58 inches long to fit securely around your body. Plus its hand-molded loops will snugly but handily hold in place most popular-size bullets, including .30/.30, .30/.06, and .45 handgun slugs.

You insist you always refuse "wet" missions, no matter how adamant the boss is? Use Bandolier on hunting trips . . . or as a distinctive fashion accessory.

Price: $65.

Supplier: Bianchi Gunleather.

BMF Activator

We haven't covered automatic weapons—guns that fire nonstop at a single pull of the trigger—because they are flatly illegal. Not so the BMF Activator, a cranklike device that attaches to a standard semiautomatic .22 rifle's trigger and transforms it into a rapid-firing behemoth.

With the Activator installed—a simple process that takes minutes—there's no longer a need to squeeze the trigger for each shot. Instead, you turn the Activator's crank

. . . and each revolution fires the rifle four times. Get good at it and soon enough you'll be firing twenty rounds *per second*—up to twelve hundred rounds every minute (which is a theoretical maximum; no conventional magazine stocks more than 25 to 50 bullets).

Made of plastic and adaptable to any .22, the Activator works for both right- and left-handed operation. Plus it's been certified legal by the federal Bureau of Alcohol, Tobacco, and Firearms. So with the Activator in place, your rifle becomes an updated Gatling gun and a legal one to boot.

Price: $19.95.

Supplier: BMF Activator.

Scribe

Ask, insist, howl, even beg for one chance to write that last note to your loved ones. The gun may be poised at your temples, but even the cruelest captors will relent. That will be *their* last action, ever, if your "pen" is the Scribe.

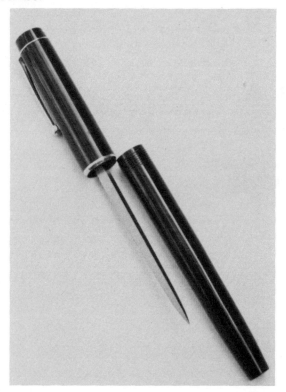

It does not write, although it is a conventional large-barrel ball-point pen. Or, rather, it is a genuine ball-point housing. Inside there is no ink, however. The Scribe draws blood, not pictures. Its innards are a needle-pointed and razor-sharp 2½-inch knife blade. The "pen" barrel is this knife's safety scabbard, and a quick twist of the cap frees this honed weapon for instant use.

An ideal backup weapon, the Scribe neatly, unobtrusively sits in a shirt or suit pocket, where it will attract no notice—until the instant you thrust it into service. And then it will get your point across. Painfully.

Price: $30.

Supplier: ASP.

Bali-Song

It is flatly illegal in its native Phillipines—a clue that its lyrical name is misleading. Its master designer also created the menacing sword used by Arnold Schwarzenegger in *Conan the Barbarian*. And its prototype was used by an ancient warrior to dispatch some twenty-nine enemies in a few fell swoops. Bali-Song is not a bird, a flower, or a restaurant. It is, quite simply, the Rolls-Royce of folding knives.

Inspired by a classical martial arts weapon, today's Bali-Song is manufactured to exacting contemporary standards. The blade is top-grade stainless steel.

But it is the handle—or rather, the handles—that is unique. Bali-Song features rotating twin handles that swing apart, exposing the blade. Grip one handle, and the other whirls out to be used as a whip or club, if the lethal thrust of sharp steel isn't needed. And if it is, grip one or both handles—it's balanced for both methods—and be confident that it will do what knives are known for doing, and splendidly.

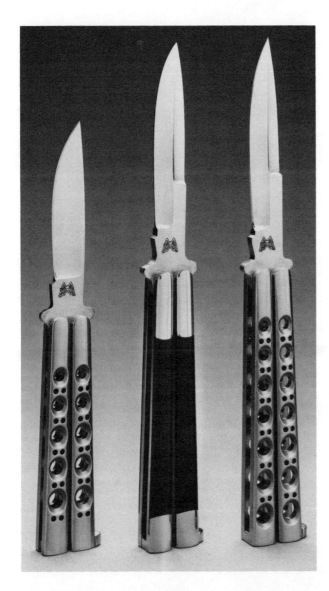

A full range of stock and custom blades and handles are available. Total knife length, blade and handle included, extends from 3 inches to 9, depending upon your choice.

Price: $175 (customized options can raise the cost to $225 and higher).

Supplier: Bali-Song.

Escort

The man stubbornly refuses to see your point. You have tried reason, persuasion, cajolery, entreaty—to no avail. He flatly refuses to budge from his opposition to your plans. If he was a friend, he is now an enemy. If he had been an enemy, he is now a deadly one. He is an obstacle, a threat; the morality and logic of the field make it so. And you know what you have to do. Your Escort can be counted on to get your final offer understood . . . and your point very much across.

There's elegance to the Escort. Rugged, dependable, and stylishly slim, the Escort features a blued-steel, triangular-ground blade and a dark gray, nonreflective, durable, Lexan-compound handle. The overall length is a small but potently effective 7 inches, which makes the Escort an easily carried—and hidden—weapon. For maximum safety and stealth a sheath for carrying this weapon on your arm or leg is included.

Price: $25 (an optional belt sheath is available at $6).

Supplier: ASP.

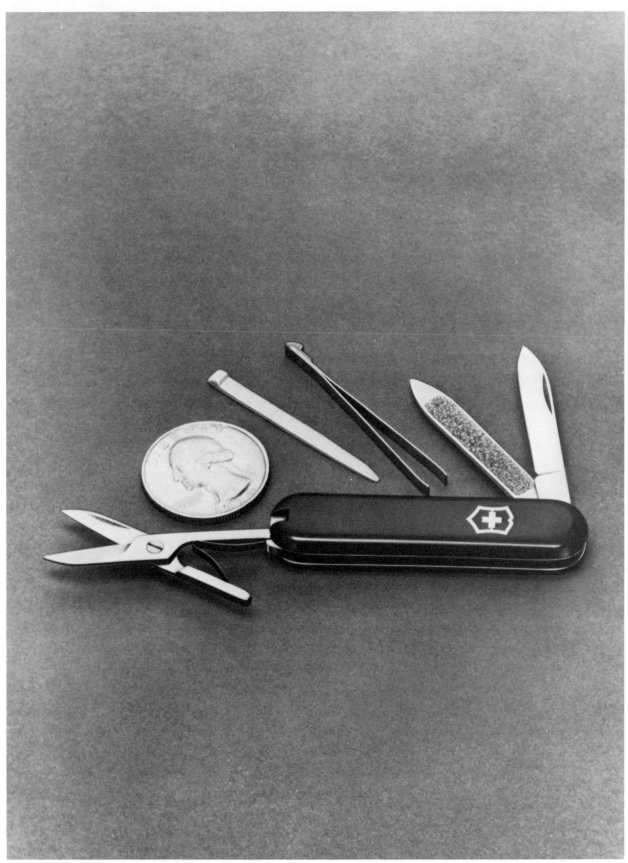

SWISS ARMY KNIFE

Classic Pocket Knives

It may be a spy's one indispensable tool. You need to snip a dangling piece of telltale telephone tap wire? Rearrange shoddy sailboat rigging for that swift escape? Trim a conspicuously misplaced eyebrow hair? Dispatch an enemy?

The classic multiblade pocket knife is the tool that can do it all. Pick wisely and you've got an array of blades plus a handsome package. Go Swiss, for instance, and tote a miniature Swiss Army knife that's right at home amid a pocketful of change but still features a utility blade, scissors, nail file, tweezers, and even a toothpick. And it's still no longer than 3 inches.

The devil with the Swiss, you snort; chocolatiers do not knife-crafters make. Debate that as you wish; another fine choice is to ally yourself with the English by buying an official British military knife. In the bargain you'll get the most versatile pocket-rigging knife around. Satin-finished stainless steel makes this knife gleam. But it's the blades that make it work. Included are a rope-cutting blade, a marlin spike for splicing, a bottle opener, a can opener, a screwdriver, a shackle key, and a lanyard shackle. All in a 3¾-inch knife that's lightweight and will comfortably fit in any pocket, designer jeans included.

Good show—but something, well, with a trace more elegance is what you're after? Try the Gentleman's Knife. Just 3 inches and a paperweight 1½ ounces, this stainless-steel knife features a 2-inch razor-keen main blade, scissors, and, for the crowning touch, a buit-in file for grooming fingernails.

Prices: Swiss Army Knife—$13.95.
British Rigging Knife—$32.95.
Gentleman's Knife—$18.95.

Supplier: Brookstone.

BRITISH RIGGING KNIFE

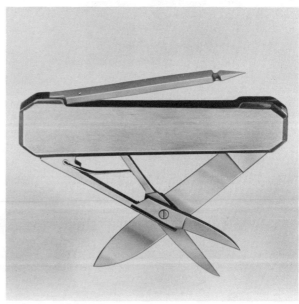

GENTLEMAN'S KNIFE

Puukko Knife

It is ugly, and it's never subtle. That is not a Puukko's breeding. It's no tool for delicate diplomacy. But flash a Puukko at your foe and he will not doubt the gravity of your intent. Because this is a knife made for deep, final stabs.

The traditional blade of no-nonsense Finnish outdoorsmen, hunters, and sailors, the Puukko features a 4-inch scalpel-sharp blade of high-carbon stainless steel. It's a strong blade, one that will resist bending even when doing the heaviest and dirtiest work. And this knife's tang—the connection that marries the blade to the handle—extends the entire length of the 4-inch black-nylon handle for assured, maximum strength.

The sheath is leather. A bear paw's emblem is stamped into it, telegraphing the ferocity of the Puukko's intent.

Price: $29.95.

Supplier: Brookstone.

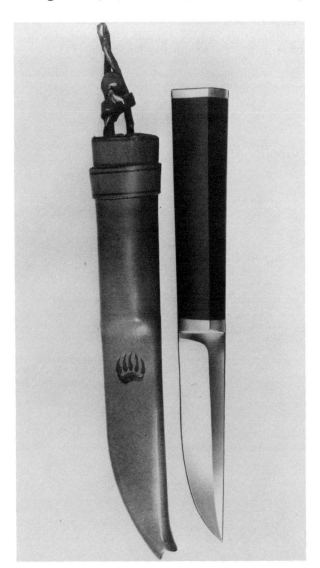

Shoulder Rig

It hangs low—just low enough to be well within reach of your lightening-fast hands. This knife shoulder harness has learned its lethal lesson from manufacturers of pistol

holsters—and why not? If the position works for handguns, it will work for knives, too.

But don't stick just any old blade in this shoulder rig. Gravity will play cruel tricks on you—and crueler ones on your feet. Take cautious note: The knife handle hangs downward, the optimun position for quick grabbing—but not for your nether digits, unless your knife comes equipped with a sheath incorporating a restraining strap. Omit that strap and you're in for a lesson in the inexorability of Newtonian physics, a lesson sure to be more pointed than an apple.

Need advice on what kind of knife to slide into this rig? The supplier recommends the Gerber Mk. I, Command Series, and Guardian blades. All feature sheaths with classic boot/belt clips for safe insertion into this black nylon harness. And for the forgetful, adapters and instructions are included with every order.

Price: $9.50.

Supplier: ASP.

Nicest Hatchet Ever Made

Something is amiss; drastically wrong. It was supposed to be a secret vacation, just a pleasant weekend outing in your log-cabin hideaway. But someone must have leaked your whereabouts, because when you awoke in the morning you found the windows and doors—all of them—cemented over. From the outside. And you are inside, with food, fuel, and oxygen all running out.

That's the idea, of course. The other side wants this death to be prolonged, miserable so that the rest of the men and women in the service will see what they are up against . . . and maybe have a change of heart.

Lucky for the service—and luckier for you—you have the nicest hatchet ever made with you. That's what the supplier calls this tool. And the claim is backed by the hatchet's specifications: one-piece construction, using solid forged steel; curved-for-comfort handle that's covered with leather; handy 13 inches long, with a 3$\frac{1}{4}$-inch cutting edge that's hardened to Rockwell C38-42 for lasting sharpness; plus a sheath that easily attaches to your belt for safe storage; and a total weight of 1$\frac{3}{4}$ pounds.

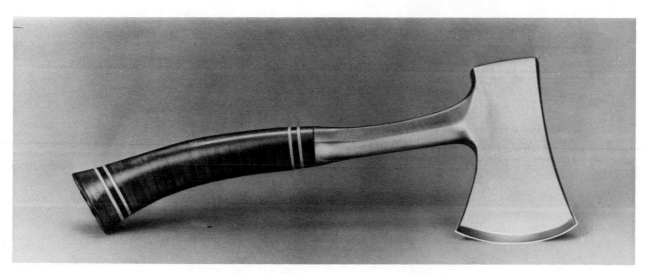

But stop admiring this hatchet, good as it is. Get busy chopping your way out of this tomb. Later on, when you're safe, take comfort in your purchase of this superb hatchet . . . and more comfort in the knowledge that your great-great-great-grandchildren, too, will enjoy this same tool when it's their turn to enlist in the service. Indeed, with that bequest in mind, you may choose to be generous—toss in a matching hammer—"the nicest hammer ever made"—and get a discount when you purchase the pair.

Price: $23.95 ($38.95 for the hatchet plus hammer; hammer alone is $17.95).

Supplier: Brookstone.

Bandit

"Have you got the time, Mac?"

You know that's the prelude. This game is not new to you, because you know it's played out in the spy haunts of Berlin and the streets of Manhattan. It is an old ruse, but it remains effective, which is why it endures.

Go ahead: Check your watch. Take your eyes off the man, lower your head a notch, and focus your vision on your timepiece. Boom! He will use your inattentiveness to destroy you.

But not if you have the Bandit, a combination knife scabbard and watchband that's worn on the inside of your forearm. Yes, that's a real watch on the Bandit, and the knife is real and sharp, too. So when you're asked for the time, by all means oblige—but keep a hand ready to dive for the knife in case the man has more than hours and minutes on his mind.

Price: $18.50 (black only; in a range of sizes, from 6½ inches to 8 inches. Watch and knife *not* included.

Supplier: ASP.

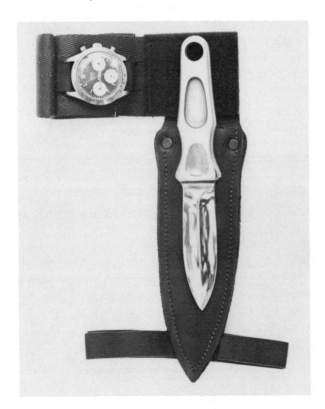

Arkansas Stone Set

You know about the Amazon: the creepy-crawlies, endless snakes, vines gone berserk, hungry plants that devour humans in their lush strangulating greenness. You remember Arnold, the agency's up-and-comer who got his final comeuppance when a damn mad voodoo lily swallowed him up. Arnold was never seen again. He simply disappeared. It sounds nuts, you admit. You don't talk about it, not with people who've never been to the Amazon. They would not understand. You do.

That is why when you pack for the trip, despite the premium on weight economy in jungle luggage, you check and double-check to make sure you are bringing your Arkansas Stone Set. No, it's not that you want to bring your own rocks to hurl at the natives and their plants. It's that this is the world's finest knife sharpening set. With three whet-

stones in all, one's for general-purpose sharpening, a second handles finer honing, and the third takes care of the blade that must be razor sharp. Chisels, machetes, knives, even scalpels—all respond to the Arkansas Stone Set's sharpening magic. So whether it's for jungle uses or urban street fighting, the Arkansas Stone Set can do the job.

Each stone in the set is a large 6 inches by 2 inches by ½ inch for long-term sharpening reliability. The trio comes packed in a redwood box, with each stone lodged in its own covered compartment. Total box size is 23 inches by 4½ inches for portability—or convenient storage in a kitchen, den, or workroom.

Price: $66.50 (a set featuring smaller stones costs $40.95).

Supplier: Brookstone.

Diamond Sharpening Rod

There is nothing—*nothing*—more humiliating than prodding a recalcitrant foe with a knife blade and having him respond with a sneering giggle. That's not the way it's supposed to go, and it simply will not do. Let that stubbornly mum witness laugh at you and soon enough the hysteria will cascade throughout the service. "Dullard," friends and foes alike will snicker behind your back.

Halt that contempt before—let us hope it is before—it even starts.

A diamond sharpening rod proves the seriousness of your intent. Its sparkle is ample to silence even the most mocking enemy,

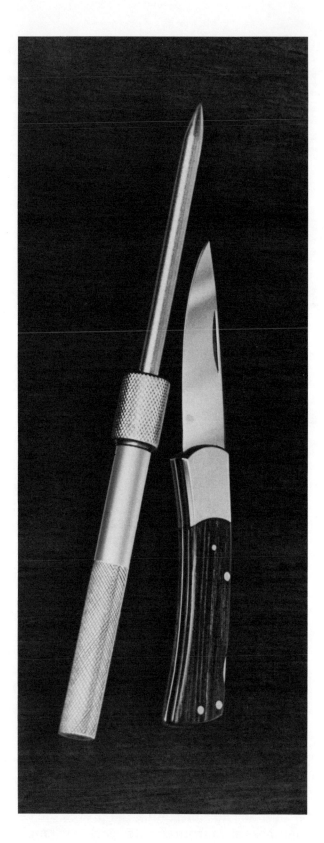

because there is no better knife sharpener than diamond.

Remember that fresh loaf of sourdough that defied you? Or was it when your knife was too dull to slice through the bindings that held your trussed feet immobile?

Never again. Whenever a razor-sharp edge is called for, just whip out this genuine diamond sharpening rod and hone away. Because diamond is the hardest material around, this tool, with its millions of microscopic diamond facets, gives your knife, ax— anything with an edge—the sharpest blade around. A few quick strokes is all it takes— and this is definitely an instance when a stroke in time saves nine, ninety, and more.

A compact 3½ inches long, the diamond rod conveniently slides into its solid brass handle for storage when not in use. But this tool's versatility—in the kitchen, the shop, and the field—assures that it will be much in use.

Price: $19.95.

Supplier: Brookstone.

The Commando Crossbow

Yours is a mission that must proceed in silence. That requirement is inflexible; there can be no hedging. It's a black job, the wettest work around, and it has to be accomplished at a distance. That rules out a knife. Ditto a gun, because no silencer is really silent.

Your choice of weapon? There is but one: the self-cocking commando crossbow, the ultimate in archery. Forget those feeble gym classes of yesteryear. This bow is not a toy, not a nature duffer's plaything. It's a lethal weapon coveted by police, survivalists, and

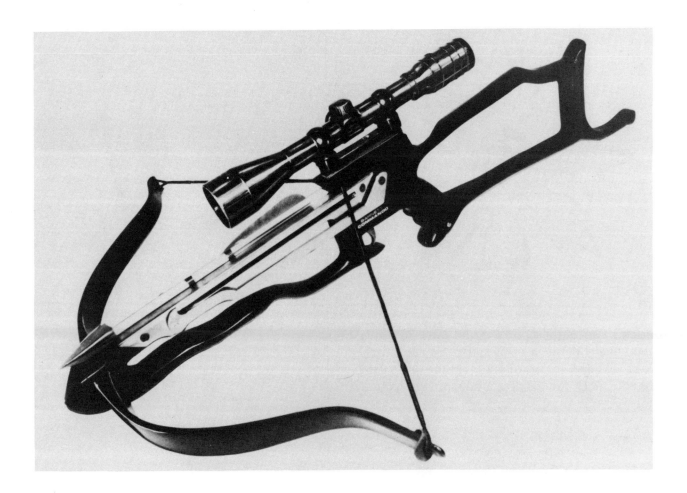

espionage agents forced to work without a sound.

Noiseless as this crossbow is, its punch is still a powerful one as it effortlessly produces a muscular 175 pounds in draw weight plus a deadly aim that's assured by its steel sights. Legal almost everywhere, this professional crossbow is an able substitute for a gun—and in the right hands it may even be better than a firearm.

Price: $385 (aluminum shaft arrows with barbed or broad tips cost $4.25–$4.50 apiece).

Supplier: Brigade Quartermasters.

Shuriken

It is pretty enough to wear on a necklace and sharp enough to slice through a neck. That's the menacing beauty of the shuriken, an eight-point star that's much favored by kung-fu adepts and other martial artists.

As with much Orientalia, the shuriken combines an alluring appearance with a profoundly logical design. The eight-point configuration is not an arbitrary, haphazard choice. Look closely at the shuriken. Note that it's extremely light weight, at most an ounce or two (depending on the precise metal used). It's tiny, too—2 inches to 4 inches in diameter; perhaps ⅛-inch thick. But throw it however you like, if it hits the target, it *will*

stick. The eight points make sure of that. And every point is razor sharp. So the shuriken is good for a relaxing game of Asian darts . . . or for getting a sharp edge over a foe.

Prices: $.79–$5.95.
Target Board—$9.95.
Vinyl Carrying Case—$1.95.

Supplier: Asian World of Martial Arts.

Sai

It is pronounced like a *sigh*—but it's your opponent who will do all the sighing when you're armed with a sai. A short (21½ inches), swordlike truncheon, the sai was originally developed on Okinawa as a kind of pitchfork, but martial artists rapidly grasped this weapon's keen potential in close-quarters combat.

Take a proven page from the Oriental practices: Carry one sai in each hand and a third inside your belt and you'll begin to understand why similarly armed Okinawans never feared intruders. In skilled hands the sai is extraordinarily versatile. Use it, for

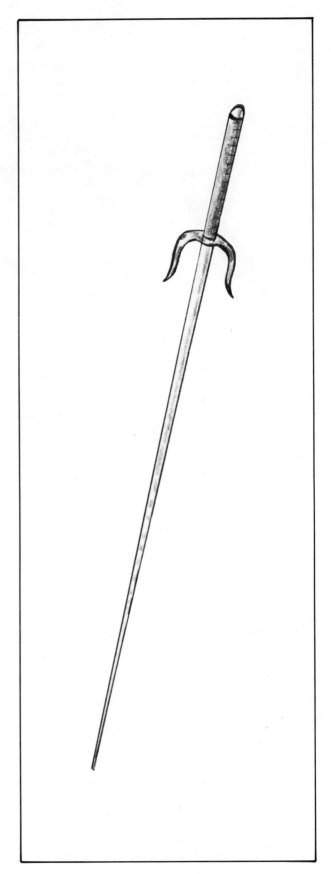

instance, to trap a foe's arm between the main blade and one of the shorter prongs on the handle. Or just jab the point into the enemy's foot and let him squirm while he is pinned to the ground. As a still sterner measure, apply the sai against one of the body's sensitive pressure points (like the carotid artery in the neck), and your antagonists will fast become putty in your hands.

You may have thought the sai was simply a stubby sword. But you've won without even resorting to the sai's razor-sharp point. Although that *is* always there if more subtle measures fail.

Price: $32.95.

Supplier: Mantis.

Nunchaku

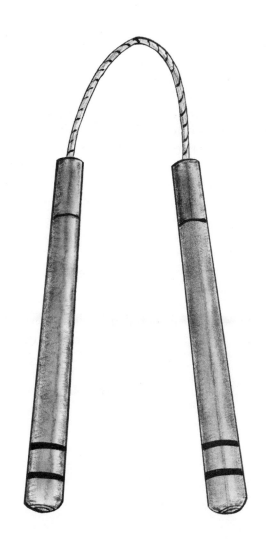

Its appearance is suggestively sinister; its uses are just as sinister. Know how to use a nunchaku—an Asian device consisting of two foot-long sticks fastened together by a chain or chord—and it can be a tool for flailing grain. That's what its inventors, Okinawan farmers, meant it to do. But don't be deceived by the bucolic-seeming man dressed in overalls who's toting a nunchaku. *Nobody* uses it on farms anymore. Not since the legendary Bruce Lee imaginatively and murderously displayed the nunchaku in *Enter the Dragon* and *Game of Death.*

Go ahead, hoist a nunchaku in your hands. The weight is light. Just 3 ounces for plastic versions, a bit more for rubber, maple and tough cocobolo hardwood models.

Now grasp only one of the paired sticks; let the other dangle. Gently swing the weapon. Notice the universal joint: The force you put into the stick you hold in your hands is directly and powerfully translated into the freely moving stick. Go faster . . . faster. The nunchaku soon is whistling, menacingly slashing through the air. Hit a foe with a nunchaku that's moving at full tilt and a staggering 1600 pounds of force will be generated at the point of impact. Many bones break when subjected to 10 pounds of force. Nearly all bones splinter when slammed with three quarters of a ton of concentrated power.

Or forget the raw power and use the nunchaku as a tool of artistic persuasion. Move quickly and slip the connecting cord around an enemy's neck. Give a tug, a twist, and be assured: This is one foe who is prepared to listen to your reasoning. Because as long as you keep him ensnared, he is going nowhere. The nunchaku's ruggedness ensures his continuing compliance, since he now is ripe for strangulation or worse.

Ideal—and certainly ferocious—as the nunchaku might seem, there are drawbacks. For one, arduous training is a prerequisite for its skilled use. Pick up a pistol and very little knowledge is required to coax a boomingly homicidal slug out of the barrel. Not so with a nunchaku. Delicate kata—regimented moves not unlike dance steps—are studied for months, even years before a savvy martial artist would begin to attempt to deploy a nunchaku in combat. Learning and mastering the technique simply is not simple.

But the effort is worth it. Witness Bruce Lee's indisputable and menacing skill. A nunchaku once mastered is noiseless, and as lethal as a gun.

Yet that's the second hitch. Many states now treat the nunchaku as a regulated weapon—no different, that is, from a gun. So check your local laws.

Prices: Plastic Nunchaku—$2.50.
Hard Rubber Nunchaku—$8.95.
Maple Nunchaku—$12.95
Cocobolo Nunchaku—$14.95.
Vinyl Carrying Case—$1.95.
Basic Kata Poster—$1.49.

Supplier: Asian World of Martial Arts.

Samurai Swords

The scarred man refuses to take "no" for an answer. He has hounded you for days, and this time has followed you home. His incessant threats trail your every step. Quick, leap inside your door and just as rapidly grab your samurai sword. One wave of this gargantuan blade and the scarred man will be on his way . . . and out of yours.

It was *Shogun* that made the point. But you can make it as keenly with your own samurai sword. No, it's not the ultimate in concealed weaponry; the wakizashi (short sword) is 27 inches and the katana (long

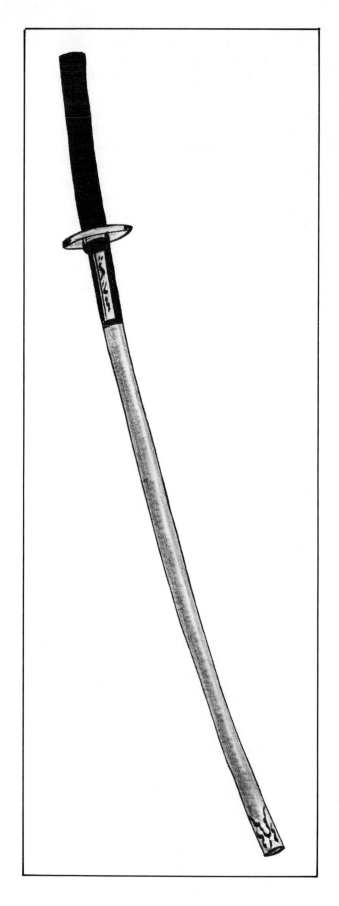

sword) is 40 inches. But it is the samurai sword's very length that engenders its fearsome mystique. It's a weapon meant for brazen, open warfare, and the sharp, tempered-steel blade plus rugged construction make it fit for the toughest, nastiest combat. Yet because of that no-nonsense reputation, a samurai sword will win many encounters by its visual impact alone: Would you want to tangle with one?

Besides, it *is* decorative. Delicate inlays and elaborate engravings are common on many models, and that makes the samurai sword an esthetic—if still eminently practical—way to introduce a smidgeon of Orientalia to home or office.

Prices: Wakizashi—$89.95.
　　　　 Katana—$109.95.

Supplier: Dolan's Sports.

Bianchi Magic Wand

The drum major gambols down the parade line. You eye him as he comes nearer and nearer the head of state. His baton twirling grows more feverish . . . and that's when you jump into action. Onlookers gasp as you swiftly tackle him and force him to the ground. They gasp all the louder when you demonstrate the brutal power of the drum major's "baton" by turning it against him and throttling this agent from the other side into hazy submission.

Thwack heads, coconuts, trees as hard as you wish. This is a baton that can take it. And dish it out. It's a Bianchi Magic Wand, one more favored by police than drum majors and majorettes, because this 26-inch baton is hollow aluminum for strength and lightweight (15 ounces) for fast striking actions. There's a rubber grip for nonslip use, and the finish is bright black for deceptive handsomeness.

Don't believe that's the recipe for a menacingly strong club? Had you ever been bashed with one during a 1960s demonstration, you would rethink your doubts—and gingerly rub your head in pained recollection.

Price: $23.50.

Supplier: Bianchi Gunleather.

Blackthorn Walking Cane

Designed for officers and gentlemen, this sturdy, virtually unbreakable walking stick is not for the lame alone. Stylish enough to do Bianca Jagger proud, the Irish Root Blackthorn is deceptively versatile.

Remember those airport metal detectors? Field frisks by friendly and hostile agents alike? In the most sensitive situations—the ones where a weapon is most needed—a gun or a knife will be sniffed out fast. But you needn't go unarmed—or "naked," as they say in the trade. Go fashionably attired instead. Dressed to the nines. Or tens. Wear a tux—or lamé if you'd like. That's not the point. The Walking Stick is—because its meter-plus length and hard, strong construction assure that it will always be a willing weapon in beating off everything from annoying animals through pesty ruffians and vicious assailants. Just one dapper smash with this cane and they will know that, dressed for the ballroom or not, action is always your calling card.

Popular with regimental officers in Her Majesty's service, the Blackthorn Cane is also a handy exercise aid and a forceful pointer—one that is ignored at the scoffer's peril.

So do it in style—but be ready no matter what "it" is. Include a stout cane in your martial wardrobe and you will be.

Price: $30.

Supplier: Brigade Quartermasters.

CRIMINALISTICS: FINDERS KEEPERS

IT STARTED WITH GOOD NEWS. *Aristotle Onassis, the Greek shipping tycoon and, later, husband to Jacqueline Kennedy, had persuaded the Saudi royal family to grant him a virtual monopoly on the marine transportation of Saudi Arabian oil. The Jiddah Agreement was the name of the 1954 deal, and with it in his pocket, Onassis stood to earn millions of dollars, maybe more.*

But the Jiddah Agreement, by its very nature, threatened the overturn of the multinational oil companies' profitable stranglehold on Saudi oil. And it struck at the crux of the oil business, the crux first discerned by John Rockefeller when that early oil baron recognized that oil in the ground is worthless and the company that transports oil from the ground to its consumers is the company that holds all the cards.

So it was no surprise that this Onassis coup enraged many. What was a surprise was the severity of the reaction. In short order "confidential" papers surfaced "showing" that Onassis had won the pact because he bribed a key Saudi; Onassis was arrested in the United States on a laundry list of hollow charges; the Greek found himself accused by the international press of wantonly murdering protected whale species; ships belonging to Onassis were summarily seized—on trumped-up charges—wherever they docked. The pretty apple, Onassis was discovering, harbored a worm.

Another worm surfaced, too, before this affair played out. Spyridon Catapodis was his name, and his was an incredible story. By profession a deal broker, Catapodis claimed he had served Onassis as a go-between with the Arabs and had a contract attesting to this—along with Onassis's agreement to share the proceeds with him. As he produced the papers for public scrutiny,

Catapodis sniveled that there was one little hitch: Onassis, the wily devil, had signed the contracts with disappearing ink, and that was why the signature was blank. Nothing better reveals the sorry state of Onassis's affairs than the fact that the public embraced Catapodis's side in this wrangle—although courts later thudded Catapodis's resulting lawsuits into the nearest trash can.

That, as it turned out, was where the Jiddah Agreement wound up, too. Onassis, even though he defeated Catapodis, glimpsed the magnitude of the odds against him and threw in the towel. The pact was voided by "mutual consent." And, incidentally, still unfolding revelations trace the architecture of Onassis's travails during this dim era to the CIA and Richard Nixon, then Vice President of the United States.

Are we to ape Onassis and rapidly toss in the towel, too? Not yet. Not with this chapter's array of precautions on our side: precautions like invisible inks, handcuff keys (you'll never be locked in again), chemical dye markers, and lock-picking paraphernalia.

Invisible Inks For Secret Writings

Now you see it, now *they* don't. That's the full story of invisible ink and the secret writings they make possible.

Write a letter and you're using a technology the Egyptians gave us six thousand years ago when, somewhere along the Nile, clever souls produced the first visible ink. Not long after that, Philo of Byzantium, a scientist who toiled in the employ of ancient Greece's military, made a dramatic improvement on this technology. He concocted a way to write military communiqués that could not be captured by the other side, even if the couriers were intercepted. Philo's technique? An invisible ink made from nuts, using a formula that was durable enough and good enough to serve George Washington well during the Revolutionary War.

Look at a letter written in Philo's nut-based ink and you'll see a blank page—a page that remains blank unless you're among the cognoscenti. How to make that message jump into visibility? The rule of thumb is this, and it works with all organic-based colorless inks: apply heat. Careful, now—apply too much heat and the paper, too, goes up in flames. Use exactly the right amount and the ink burns. What's left is a carbon-based substance, a natural by-product of combustion, that transforms the once-hidden message into a visible one.

Where to find organic inks? Search your kitchen. Milk, lemon juice, and vinegar do fine. Your cupboards are bare? Saliva and urine work in a pinch. And the technique for using all these "inks" is simple. Your tools are the fluid itself, cotton swabs (ones with wooden sticks are best), and a soft cloth. Gently rub a piece of paper with the cloth, write the message with a swab, let the ink dry, and conclude with a final rubbing to avoid the telltale presence of fluid tracks on the paper. Congratulations; the secret is written . . . and hidden.

You've spotted a flaw? Isn't a carefully carried *blank* page suspicious in itself? Indeed. That's why, to avoid detection by the other side, many secret writers painstakingly splice their confidential messages between innocuous lines of a conventional letter written in visible ink.

Even so, the heat test still is easily applied whenever doubt arises . . . which leads to the development of second-generation invisible inks like Edmund Scientific's, which only pops into visibility when illuminated by a *black* light. And if yours is a more personal or intimate message, there's invisible body paint that works the same way.

Prices: Invisible Ink (1 pint)—$14.95.
Body Paint (4½ ounces)—$4.95.
Black Light (fixture included)—$54.95 (bulb alone is $30.00).

Supplier: Edmund Scientific.

Chemical Snare Kits

There is a thief at work in your office. Day after day you return to work only to find valuables and personal letters stolen, keepsakes gone. Melvin Tuna, you've no doubt, is the culprit. He has the unnerving habit of oozing his odiferous self into your sights and silently mouthing what he considers little endearments at you. Melvin, however, is the Chief's second cousin once-removed, so decorous caution is required. You must be cetain that when you level your accusation, you've got the thief red-handed.

A Chemical Snare Kit does the job. Treat the tempting objects on your desk and shelves with its special stains which, at a touch, adhere to a perpetrator's skin. These stains aren't so visible as to frighten Mr. Tuna away before he gets down to business:

The potions, powders, and pastes in this kit come in various colors, which can be mixed to match the color of your marked objects. So Melvin will be marked the next time he fondles your belongings. "Out, damned spot!" he may whimper as he rushes to wash off the offending pigment. But he will only intensify his guilt: Water sharpens these stains into brighter hues. Only your kit can remove the marks, so you're sure to identify the guilty party.

This one is too clever? Camouflaged the stains may be, but he'll sniff out the ruse? Employ the Invisible Trap Kit, a potpourri of ultraviolet-sensitive powders and sprays. Invisible to the naked eye, when viewed under a UV light, they instantly pop into clear and incriminating colors.

Prices: Visible Stain Kit—$93.
Invisible Trap Kit (UV light included)—$130.

Supplier: LEA.

Bianchi Handcuffs

You've got an assailant or intruder subdued. How to keep him that way while you summon help? Snap on a pair of Bianchi Handcuffs, and struggle as the ruffian might, he will remain securely, snugly locked up. Made of the strongest stainless steel, these police-quality cuffs withstand a half-ton and more of direct pull, and the easily employed double lock thwarts attempts at picking. Lock up a thug with Bianchi Handcuffs, in other words, and he is bound to stay locked up until you determine to release him—for which two keys, plus complete instructions, are provided.

Price: $21 (a black leather holster, designed for convenience and as a shield against dampness, is optional; the cost is $15).

Supplier: Bianchi Gunleather.

Thumbcuffs

You need the subduing power of handcuffs, but on covert missions you cannot afford their weight, bulk, or easy visibility? Thumbcuffs are your answer. Miniature for ready concealment in pants or shirt pockets yet made of rugged chrome-plated steel, thumbcuffs provide sure locking power. Just force a suspect to interlock his fingers and—snap—the thumbcuffs comfortably fit over his thumbs and definitely lock his hands into a benign togetherness. The suspect scoffs when you suggest the finger interlocking? Snap the thumbcuffs on anyway; the lock still holds, and his chances of escape remain slim. Only his pain is greater . . . and it will

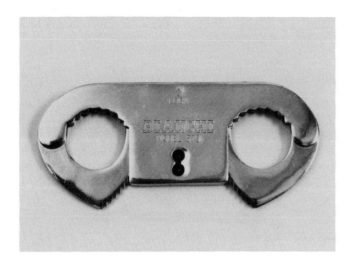

remain greater until he gets the wisdom of your message and knits his fingers together.

Price: $12.

Supplier: Bianchi Gunleather.

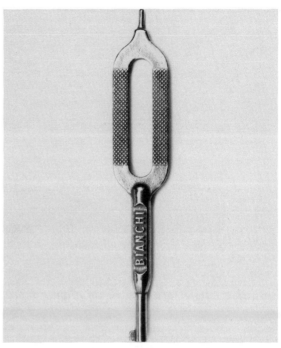

Handcuff Key

You groggily shake your head as you gradually emerge from unconsciousness. But you want to shut your eyes again tight when you glance around. You're held in a dark, dank, authentic torture chamber. The rack beckons.

You jerk yourself off the floor, and abruptly stumble back down. You look and sadly see the handcuffs that bind your arms and legs together. It takes little imagination to piece together what awaits you.

Except you have the means to rewrite the story—right in your pocket—because an indispensable tool in your work kit is a heavy-duty handcuff key, a nearly universal model that fits and unlocks Bianchi, S & W, Peerless, and most other standard police and civilian handcuffs and thumbcuffs.

A tiny 3½ inches long for easy concealment, this stainless-steel key features a slot-

ted keyhole to permit use with gloved hands and in difficult circumstances—circumstances, that is, like yours.

Just insert the key (do it with your mouth if need be), and seconds later and no matter how tightly you had been bound, you're free. And prepared for fresh action.

Price: $5.50.

Supplier: Bianchi Gunleather.

Lock-Picking Tools

Your hours of hard work have finally paid off. Night after night you've trailed the other side's ace courier, and finally she's led you to their base. Just inside the door you know you'll find all their secrets . . . but between you and that cache stands a rugged locked door and the bruiser of a safe they're sure to have hidden their valuables in. You can't unleash force to batter your way in; that

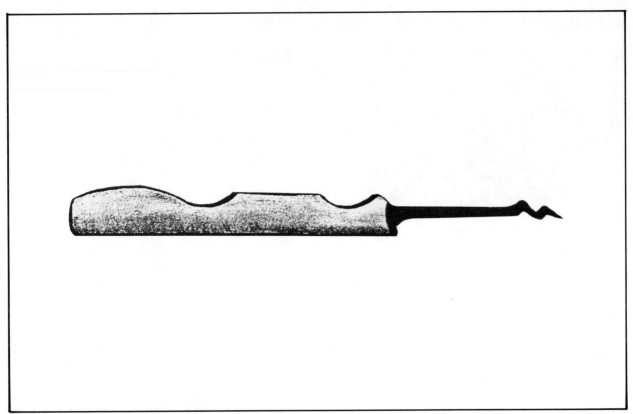

BELSAW INSTITUTE'S BASIC LOCKPICK

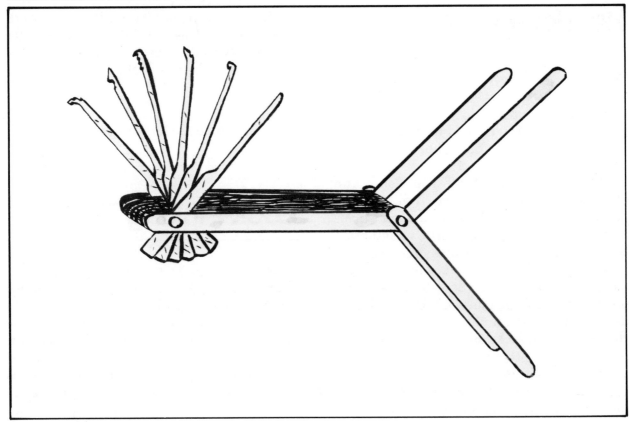

PIX-EX

would bestir this sleepy neighborhood. There would be calls to the police, and explanations you'd have to conjure up quickly.

Save your words; pick your way into the other side's fortress; or through any other locked door. No muscles are required; virtually no noise is made. But if you have the right tools and know how to use them, you're *never* locked out. Just insert the proper pick into the target lock, jiggle a bit to reposition the pins and tumblers, and pop—the door opens. As simple as that. So it's a sure snap to gain entry to the other side's lair . . . and just as easy to get into your own home, even when you've left your keys on the nightstand or locked them inside your car.

Now it's coming back to you—that freezing night spent waiting for a locksmith? Here's the alternative:

Start with Pik-Quick. Packed in a convenient see-through plastic carrying pouch, Pik-Quick provides an assortment of eight hardened blue steel picks, and that means there's one for opening nearly every conventional lock. Picks are lightweight, too, with color-coded handles for ease of use and convenience.

Pik-Ez is more convenient still. Only 4 inches long and as comfortable to carry as a pocket knife—it even resembles Swiss Army knives—Pik-Ez is an all-in-one pick set with six built-in steel picks. And the picks are fashioned with the appropriate tooling and grooves to slice through a wide variety of locks.

Lockaid is *most* convenient, however. Shaped like a gun and much favored by law-enforcement agencies, Lockaid is specifically designed to make a mockery of the security promised by pin tumbler locks, the most frequently encountered kind of lock. Just show Lockaid that breed, and in a wink the lock is picked. That's because three extraordinary thin and sensitive "needles" (included with Lockaid) fit into the gun's barrel for instant penetration. Lockaid is guaranteed for life, and every tool in the package features a serial number to thwart thieves.

Exactly how are these tools employed in the field? Good question. You'll get a good, thorough answer by reading *Lockpicking Illustrated*. It's a detailed primer that tells precisely how locks work and the best ways to open them.

Want even more detailed schooling on locks? Enroll in Belsaw Institute's correspondence Course of Professional Locksmithing. Picking is *not* the subject matter; keys, lock making, and lock installation are. But complete the thirty-lesson course (at a recommended maximum pace of five lessons monthly) and you'll be a certified pro with an expert understanding of all locks. Plus, as part of the enrollment package, Belsaw provides its students with a vast assortment of aids and tools, including picks, emergency house- and car-opening tools, master keys and code books, and practice locks. The kit's final touch is a stock of blank keys for automobile and house locks *and* a motorized key cutting machine for speedy duplication of existing keys and fast creation of new ones.

Before plunging into locks and picks, however, there's a *caveat* for you to digest. Many localities restrict possession of picking gear to licensed or student locksmiths—although one typically may qualify as a student by pursuing a course of self-instruction and "self-teaching." As a rule, too, such tools are flatly denied to convicted felons.

Prices for tools: Pix-Quick—$20.00.
Pix-Ez—$27.95.
Lockaid—$80.00.
Lockpicking Illustrated—
$3.50.

Supplier: The Larder—Survival Books.

Price for correspondence course: $479.

Supplier: Belsaw Institute.

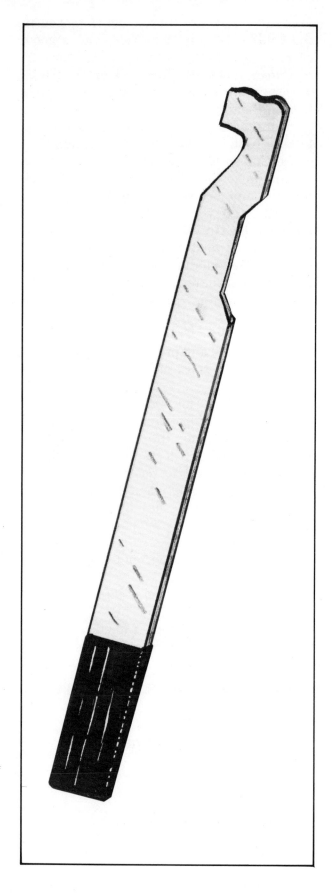

Super Slim Jim

You slam your head against the car door and mix sobs with curses. In fifty minutes you are due at Langley HQ, and here you are in Delaware, at a roadside restaurant, and now you've locked yourself out of your car. "Stupid," you chastise yourself . . . then you remember how bright you are. You open the attaché case, take out the Super Slim Jim, and seconds later you're behind the wheel, whistling and motoring down the road.

You'll never again be locked out of your car—or anyone else's, for that matter—with Super Slim Jim in your bag of tricks. It's the one way to get in that's just as good as a key. Better, in fact, because Super Slim Jim opens just about all cars. Simply slide it into the slight gap between the door and frame, wriggle around a bit until you locate the lock's operating rod, and pop—the lock jumps open. It's as simple as that, and it takes no more time to do than it does to read about it.

Super Slim Jim is thin enough at .032 of an inch thick to find its way into most cars. And at 22½ inches in length, it's convenient to carry on all missions.

Price: $9.30.

Supplier: The Larder—Survival Books.

The Escort Radar Detector

Mysticism is not your line. But clairvoyance is. Knowing what's about to happen before it does is an essential ability in your line of work. Unfortunately, despite years of practice, your extra-sensory perception is woe-

fully unreliable. Fortunately, technology is making inroads in the field of future-telling. There is now a radar detector so accurate in its ability to warn of dangers ahead that it puts poor Jean Dixon to beet-faced shame.

It is a nuisance—sometimes an embarrassment—to be speeding down the New Jersey Turnpike on the long route to Langley, Virginia, only to be stopped by the insistent whine of police sirens. There inevitably is so much explaining to do: the corpse in the trunk; the automatics in the backseat; the plastic explosives in the front. No trooper will buy your tale of a masquerade ball, and a detour to the state police barracks is just out of the question.

How to prevent it? It's obvious: Know where the police are *before* you go steaming by them. Cincinnati Microwave's Escort radar detection unit will tell you.

Escort is the latest in sophisticated, state-of-the-art detection gear. When the BMW Car Club of America put the top radar detectors to the test, Escort came out ahead by a wide margin. Ditto for the results of *Car and Driver*'s test laps.

Escort is *the* best. It's calibrated to pick up both the X and K bands of police radar—the only frequencies assigned to that purpose by the Federal Communications Commission—and it provides dual audible and visual signals whenever radar is encountered. Not even the latest in devious police tactics succeeds in foiling the wily Escort; its selectivity and wide band of operation are designed effectively to sort out false alarms while strongly targeting the real radar alerts. What's more, Escort is sensitive enough always to provide ample *advance* warning, so you've plenty of time to gradually, smoothly come down to the legal speed limit.

It is powered by your car's lighter socket, and installation is fast, with detailed instructions provided. Low levels of microwave energy are radiated by the Escort, but the manufacturer claims only negligible amounts are involved.

Price: $245.

Supplier: Cincinnati Microwave.

Special Investigations Kit

Life: sometimes it seems like an uphill battle. So be prepared to climb. The Rouse Special Investigations Kit has everything you need to get to the top—whether it's the top of a building, a mountain, a telephone pole, or a tree. All equipment is identical to the gear used by police SWAT teams, and it's much the same as the tools used by Hollywood stunt man Ron Broyles, who, tuxedo-clad, recently climbed a sixty-two-story bank building in Los Angeles. Broyles, incidentally, took four hours to reach the building's top, where he celebrated by hanging upside down and smoking a cigar.

Contents of the Rouse kit include: SWAT-style suit of clothing plus cap; kermantle rope; grappling hook; carabiners; figure-eight descender; Gibbs ascenders; gloves; Flex-Lite (which clips on SWAT suit to provide illumination and leaves both hands free); chest and seat harness; pole and tree climbers; body belt; saddle belt; safety strap; utility bag.

Price: $649.95.

Supplier: The Rouse Company.

Makeup Kit

How to become someone else? Make a list of all the elements that make you recognizable and do the opposite. If you're blond, go brunet. If you're female, go male. If you're young, go old. If you're handsome, go ugly. If you're scrawny, go beefy.

Many of the products you could use to create a new persona can be found at your local thrift shop or discount department store (wigs, clothes, material for padding, eyeglasses), but the tools of the pro are worth mentioning here.

A worthwhile investment for any spy is the #7 Character Makeup Group Kit. It contains nearly every color of nearly every substance you'd need to create nearly any disguise, as well as a basic makeup guide to teach you how to use the products. Since it all comes in a sturdy 16-by-6-by-8 inch metal box, you can take your supplies with you for on-the-spot changeovers, too.

Included in the kit are:

10 foundation colors in versatile, mixable "soft grease" for changing your basic skin color

6 face powders for setting the foundation so it won't smear and for instant skin tone change when you're in a hurry.

1 face-powder brush to whisk away any excess powder

6 puffs for applying or blending makeup

12 "soft liners," bright or deep colors for making shadows, wrinkles, and highlights

3 moist rouges for rosy cheeks, or flushes, or blushes, or sunburns, or a quaint alcoholic tinge on the nose

1 tin of "clown white" for custom lightening other makeup, to make the highlight in a highlight, or, in a pinch, for whitening your hair a bit

1 wad each "nose putty" and "derma wax" to make a hump in your nose or smooth out a scar or cover the edge of a telltale hairline

4 eyebrow pencils for—you guessed it—disguising eyebrows as well as making moles and fashion-model eyes

1 container black mascara for darkening lashes, brows, sideburns, mustaches and hairlines

2 dry rouges for reddening an area that has already been powdered

collodian, a nifty substance that contracts the skin as it dries—great for scars, scabs, and warts

liquid latex, the true miracle in your box, to make three-dimensional wrinkles; as a base for false beards and mustaches, eye pouches, new noses; or as an adhesive for other substances

7 lengths of different color crepe hair for making beards, mustaches and eyebrows

spirit gum for attaching crepe hair or doubly securing latex or nose putty

3 sizes of oxhair brushes for applying your makeup accurately

silver color spray for graying the hair

black tooth enamel for making you look like you haven't seen a dentist since 1937

paper stomps for blending your shadows and highlights

cold cream for removing all this gunk

Price: $107.

Supplier: Alcone.

Make-up in Action

To prove how easy it is to turn yourself into somebody else, we've asked two super sleuths with only fair to middling expertise in the makeup department to share their secrets. Savannah Stiletto (she's the one with the long hair and the smoldering look) and Archie Bullet (he's the one who looks deceptively like a high school senior) utterly transform themselves on a daily basis, and so can you. Since they never go anywhere without their butler, Uriah Lounge (the one with the glasses), they have to disguise him, too.

Last year the three found themselves in Monte Carlo watching a donneur who was dealing more than cards. Needing to roam the casino inconspicuously, they came up with three appropriate personas: Bubbly

ARCHIE BULLET, SUPER SLEUTH

SAVANNAH STILETTO, SUPER SLEUTH

URIAH LOUNGE, BUTLER

Miss Bunny Parton from Memphis, USA, for Savannah; trillingly Parisian Melissé Spacét for the fluent-in-French Archie; and Abdul Mon Dollah for the somewhat-difficult-to-disguise Uriah. They all fit right in; especially Uriah, who, as the sheikh, was so loaded with cash he never had to open his mouth.

To create Miss Bunny, Savannah first donned a wig and a few strategically placed pairs of socks. For her face, neck, and all other exposed skin, she used a very light foundation, with extra lightening under her cheekbones and on the bridge of her nose to make them seem broader; a mixture of black and brown eyebrow pencil for a few distinctive beauty marks and entirely different eyebrows; a smidgen of shadow under her eyes to make her look a little older, a little tireder; a hint of highlighter to make her eyes seem puffy. After outlining her mouth with pencil, she filled in the new, more generous contours with bright red lip color. She shaded her chin

ARCHIE BULLET AS MELISSÉ SPACÉT

SAVANNAH STILETTO AS MISS BUNNY PARTON

URIAH LOUNGE AS ABDUL MON DOLLAH

to make it rounder; accentuated cleavage with some shadow, highlighter and rouge; powdered the whole thing; brushed off the excess; and made up her eyes in a crescent-moon shape with pencil, liner, and mascara.

Archie's Melissé used most of the same methods and products, with a few additions. To block out any trace of five o'clock shadow, he covered his beard line with an even lighter shade of foundation before applying a pale peaches and cream base. He had to trim his eyebrows a bit but not so much that he'd look strange when the mission in Monte Carlo was over. So he blocked out the extra strands with spirit gum and derma wax, smoothing base and then liner (in a lovely leaf green shade) over his upper lid, and using a pencil to perfect the line of his remaining eyebrows.

To turn Uriah into Abdul, they attached fake nose (not included in the Alcone kit) with spirit gum, flattening the edges with latex. They used a dark base, with even darker shadows around the eyes, upper lip, and jawline. A tiny mustache made of crepe hair whiskers and a tuft under the lower lip completed the makeup.

Needless to say, the trio wandered undetected, and Miss Bunny and Melissé were able to call the donneur's hand without him ever knowing that forever after he'd be lucky to play a game of fish. Meanwhile, Uriah—or rather Abdul—cleaned up.

For their next mission, in their hometown, New York City, the three needed disguises for a stay in Times Square. Archie became Fat Lip Frankie, a welterweight who'd seen better days. Savannah decked herself out as Fat Lip's manager, Willie (The Wino) O'Toole. With enormous efforts the two pros turned Uriah into James J. Caldicott, a writer from the *Village Voice* doing a piece on the political economy of boxing.

To give Fat Lip his distinctive look, Archie used a piece of sponge wedged between his gums and lip, and with drops of spirit gum and latex deftly colored with red and

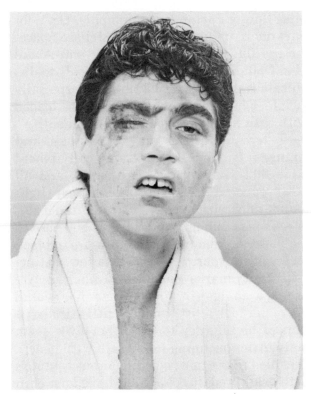

ARCHIE BULLET AS FAT LIP FRANKIE

SAVANNAH STILETTO AS WILLIE (THE WINO) O'TOOLE

URIAH LOUNGE AS JAMES J. CALDICOTT

SAVANNAH STILETTO AS MS. BEATRICE CALDICOTT-SMITH

yellowish liner, he gave himself a number of ripe pimples. He sealed his right eye with a piece made from latex and added scars and scabs with collodian. With shadow and highlighter he changed the shape of his nose slightly. And with black enamel he created an impression of a chipped tooth.

For Willie (The Wino), Savannah put blotches of spirit gum and latex all over her face to roughen the texture; added latex eye pouches; shaped a putty nose; attached crepe hair eyebrows, mustache, and whiskers; stippled (used a coarse sponge to make a pattern) several different colors of base and liner all over her face. She browned her teeth with eyebrow pencil.

For the most miraculous transformation of Uriah into James J. Caldicott, Savannah and Archie first forced Uriah to brush his teeth, take off his glasses, wash his hair and change his clothes. He was reluctant. He thought they were trying to make him look like what he termed a fruit basket. Never-

theless, he complied. Once the hair, teeth, and clothes were taken care of, all that was necessary was a trimming of the eyebrows and a warm base color to diminish Uriah's natural pallor.

Well, to make a long story short, they completed their top-secret mission in Times Square with little incident. Except for one thing . . . Uriah, as James J. Caldicott, was picked up by the police for loitering. So Savannah had to disguise herself as his mother, Ms. Beatrice Caldicott-Smith, a professor of medieval history at Columbia, in order to bail him out.

Ms. B. C.-S. was created out of a wig, some lines, a little nose putty, some slight shading, and a bit of latex crinkling around the eyes.

If the exploits of Savannah, Archie, and their butler Uriah don't convince you that becoming another person is possible, just think of the Weatherpeople, Kathy Powers (still on the FBI's most-wanted list after more than a decade), and Patti Hearst and her captors, all of whom used disguises to elude the authorities and succeeded for at least a time.

(The foregoing products are included in the basic Alcone makeup kit.)

Make Up Guides

If makeup is new to you, you might want to read a few books on the subject.

Stage Make-up by Richard Corson is the most comprehensive book on makeup ever written. It includes color charts for comparing brands, easily understood theory and history, and detailed, illustrated instructions for producing practically any final result.

The Technique of Film and Television Make-up for Color and Black and White by Vincent Kehoe concentrates on advanced techniques, many of which are particularly appropriate for real-life disguises.

Make-up for Theater, Film and Television by Lee Baygan, director of NBC's makeup department since 1966, is the newest on the market. This book includes state-of-the-art innovations as well as the step-by-step process for achieving a particular effect.

Prices: Stage Make-up—$23.95.
The Technique of Film and Television Make-up—$29.50.
Make-up for Theater, Film and Television—$22.95.

Supplier: Alcone.

False Identity Kit

When time is really of the essence and you have to change your identity instantly, just pop into a bathroom stall, open the convenient Rouse Kit carrying case, stick on one of the two mustaches, the beard, and the wig, then flush the toilet and emerge a new man. Or a man if you weren't one to begin with.

All four Rouse false identity pieces are made of 100-percent human hair for wearer comfort and reliability of disguise. The wig comes only in a dark brown hue, but the beard and mustaches are available in a range of shades (black, dark, medium, or light brown; blond; and gray). Specify color selections when ordering.

Price: $59.95.

Supplier: The Rouse Company.

Electronic Handkerchief

You're undercover. It's Mother's Day. You know her phone is tapped and connected to a voice analyzer, because they are looking hard for you. But there's a simple solution: Use the Electronic Handkerchief when you call home. It will disguise your voice so that even the voice analyzer won't be able to identify you. Your mother won't, either, but you can't have everything.

Remember the old ploy of draping a handkerchief or towel over a telephone mouthpiece to distort a voice just enough so it isn't yours, but not so much that it's incompre-

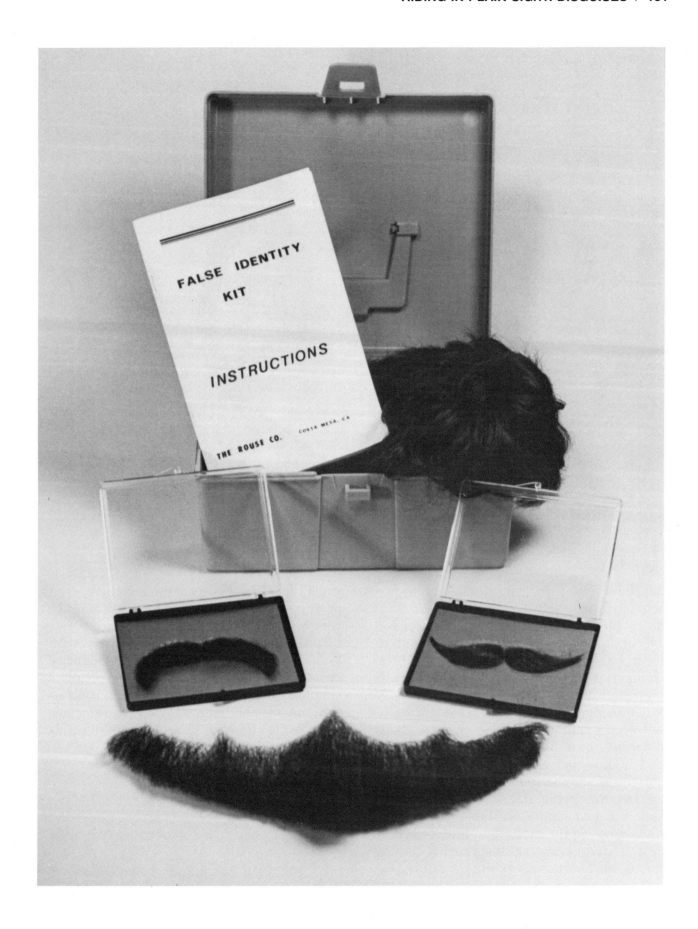

hensible? The Electronic Handkerchief is a sophisticated, high-tech updating of that hoary tactic. Precise details of the mechanical innards are kept secret by the manufacturer, but—in simplest form—what the Electronic Handkerchief does is systematically alter your natural tones into somebody else's. When using the device, you speak normally, but what comes out the other end is a wholly different voice. Yet that new voice is clear and undistorted, and no decoding is necessary for comprehension.

The Electronic Handkerchief can make Goldie Hawn sound like James Earl Jones, and James Earl Jones sound like, well, Don Knotts. It's handy for discouraging harassment—and for posing as whatever alter ego you'd like. Thwart taps, tape recorders, even prying reporters who've got a keen nose for whatever news you're up to.

All Electronic Handkerchiefs comes with a built-in, operating telephone. Identity switching is accomplished by activating a simple switch, and a separate knob controls the timbre and tone of your transformed voice while allowing for selection of multiple alter egos.

Price: $5,000.

Supplier: CCS.

Rearoscope

It resembles a novelty shop toy, but put before the right pair of eyes, the Rearoscope is a ruthless surveillance tool. Glasses with a gimmick, that is what Rearoscope is—and the gimmick is fascinatingly clever.

Consider the problem: You want to observe a suspect's movements without tipping him off to your interest. You could tail him; that would be the conventional method. Try to shadow a seasoned suspect, however, and he is sure to slip away within a pair of blocks; at the very best, and only if you are very good, he will quickly learn of your interest, and that alone will set him on a new, innocuous, and unrevealing course.

Rearoscope changes the equation—and the results. Pop on Rearoscope and what you do is walk in *front* of your quarry. No, the suspect will not believe it, either. But what Rearoscope provides is the proverbial pair of eyes in the back of your head: A high-quality optical mirror system is built into the frames. The mirrors, which work much like a car's rearview mirror (look to the side and you see what's behind you; look ahead and you see what's in front), are hidden to remain unseen by anyone except the wearer and are adjustable to provide a wide angle of rearward vision. Sneak assaults from the rear by suspects are prevented in the bargain. So no matter what is on your prey's mind or where his movements take him, wear Rearoscope and you remain in the know and a step or two ahead.

Available in a choice of frame styles, Rearoscope is made for both men and women; the lenses are impact-resistant plastic, which can be ordered clear or with gray or brown tints. A plastic case comes in the package, as does a five-year guarantee.

Price: $99. (for an extra charge, Rearoscope users who wear corrective lenses can arrange to have prescription glasses fit into the Rearoscope frames).

Supplier: LEA.

OVER THE BRINK: SURVIVALISM

IT IS NOT JUST THE OTHER SIDE *that can do you in. Nature, too, is often your enemy in espionage. And it is a nasty, formidable foe. Missions that are thoroughly, meticulously planned can go fatally awry because flooding rivers block exit routes or a foot of sudden April snow leaves you stranded deep within a hostile mountain range.*

Unlike the other side, nature and its erratic weather cannot be beaten. But it can be endured, even subdued. Survival feats are legion—stranded, shipwrecked sailors survive three months on a fragile life raft in turbulent seas; smiling teenagers emerge from under a thick mountain of snow a week after the avalanche trapped them.

Meet nature head to head, however, and it's always favored to retain the championship: It has many more lethal tricks at its disposal—until, that is, you dramatically shade the odds in your favor with tools and emergency gear designed precisely to help you survive, no matter the blackness of the skies . . . or the other side's plans.

HELP!

You're in a real jam. Like an old movie, the villain now is sneering "Curtains!" And he is not talking window hangings.

So you floor the gasoline pedal, and your car zooms away. Too soon you realize that, yes, you've lost your shadow—but you've also lost yourself. You're at a dead end. It's getting worse: Water is rapidly rising all around you; it's nearing window level. Then you see it: Those "logs" aren't trees. They are alligators, hungry ones who've tagged you as a tasty fast food.

Now what?

HELP! to the rescue. Just plug the HELP! citizen's band unit into the cigarette lighter, carefully reach outside and place the magnetic base antenna on the roof (best do something—anything—to distract the alligators while you're at it), dial emergency channel 9, and push the emergency distress button. That's it: Help will be on the way.

A portable two-way CB, HELP! features forty channels and 4 watts of power. There's a digital readout, a noise suppressor for clarity, a hand-held transmitter/receiver, and an oversize dynamic speaker—all packed in a sturdy storage case that's compact enough (12″ × 3″ × 7″) to hide under a car seat. And since HELP! installs easily and quickly, it can be toted from car to car—rental cars included—and even used aboard boats.

Price: $99.

Supplier: The Sharper Image.

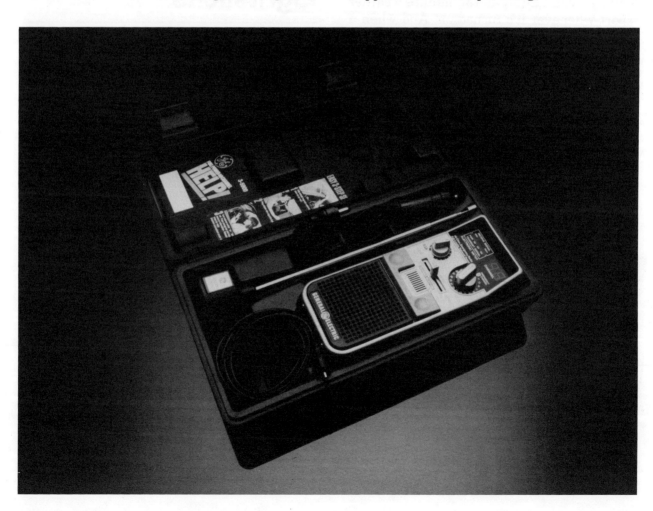

Storm Alarm Radio

You're immersed in pasting up microdots in your studio atop Mount Baldy when you're startled out of your oblivious reverie by the blare of an alarm from the Storm Alarm Radio. Instantly the local office of the National Weather Service warns of an approaching blizzard. You'd better clear out fast, because once the snow hits, there'll be no getting out for days. You'd have been stranded and missed your deadline had you waited for the evening news instead of relying on your ever-vigilant Storm Alarm Radio.

Permanently tuned to the National Weather Service frequency, the Storm Alarm Radio provides an up-to-the-minute weather report whenever it's turned on. And when a climatic calamity is approaching, the service triggers a signal that sets off the radio's alarm even if you're not listening at the time.

Small and portable at 1¼ by 5 by 3 inches, the Storm Alarm Radio weathers all conditions. It operates both on house current and a 9-volt battery, at your option.

And the Storm Alarm Radio's uses are as diverse as the weather itself. Kids like it because they get first word on school closing. Homeowners depend on it to warn of impending hurricanes, cyclones, heavy storms, and the like. Sports enthusiasts and boaters know it will keep them abreast of meteorological conditions at the quick flick of a button. And spies love it because it never lies.

Price: $44.95 (fully assembled).

Supplier: Heathkit.

Lightsticks

You prowl into the darkened room. You're sure the papers are here, and you're excited. But wait—that smell. Is it gas?

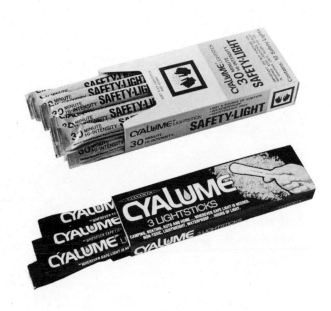

Strike a match and you would know for sure. Too sure, perhaps. Not so if it's a Lightstick that you flex. A quick bend of the thin tube and—whoosh—the yield is a heatless, flameless, luminous glow: ample light to inspect a darkened room, a cave, or under an automobile's sometimes-volatile hood.

Need a light underwater? Again it's a Lightstick at your service. And a gusting wind won't extinguish the flame.

Nontoxic and lightweight, Lightsticks last for four years on the storage shelf. In use, the Lightstick provides twelve hours of glowing yellow-green light. The thirty-minute Lightstick produces a half-hour of sharp, brilliant yellow light. Both make sure position markers in the field, and either is suitable for providing a working light.

Price: 12-hour Lightstick, $1.90; 30-minute Lightstick, $2.00.

Supplier: Brigade Quartermasters.

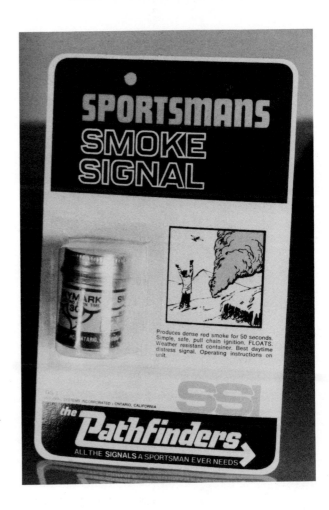

Skymark Smoke

Face it: You're lost. It's scary; terrifying, in fact. You're miles from nowhere and without a clue to your whereabouts. Every tree in the forest starts to look alike. The creaking of crickets is working on your nerves. Once-familiar trail markers blur into a meaningless sameness. No exit route pans out. But you're sure help is near; the rest of your team has got to be close by. But where? The woods play tricks on you. Your comrades are certain to be looking for you by now, but they could be over the next mountain or down in the next valley, and even so they'd never hear your anguished cries for help. That's the way woods are.

Nope; shouts won't save you. But thick clouds of spectacular orange smoke will. And with a single canister of Skymark Smoke, a quick tug on the triggering chain will deliver billows of that alerting orange smoke—a cry for help that's unmistakable and visible for miles.

Price: Available in two sizes—a 30-second smoke signal costs $3.50; the minute version sells for $5.25.

Supplier: Brigade Quartermasters.

Stormproof Map Treatment

Success: You've stolen the secret documents and you'll soon be home. But first, before you're safe, there's that quick swim across

the border river. The documents will be destroyed by water!

No, they won't. Not if you've remembered Stormproof Map Treatment. Simply paint or brush this water repellant and mildew retardant on any piece of paper, and no matter what it is—a map, blueprint, chart, birth certificate, or purloined classified documents—the paper is completely waterproofed and safe from the tsunamis, coffee spills, and drenchings in between. So swim across that river or ocean; the papers will make it intact.

Stormproof Map Treatment does not harm or alter paper characteristics; the paper is precisely as it was before treatment except now it resists water damage. Treated paper can still be marked on, written on, and erased on. And Stormproof dries fast without stiffening to allow ready folding and storage of treated documents in a dry field or a wet sea.

Price: $4.49 for a half pint; a pint container costs $7.49.

Supplier: Brigade Quartermasters.

Field & Sports Wallet

Sure, leather packs more elan, and any other manner of billfold would make a strikingly wrong impression when it's time to ante up for a dinner at Maxim's or Lion D'Or. But what's right at a party in Paris or Washington may be all wrong when yours is covert fieldwork. And that is definitely true when wallets are the issue.

Try this experiment: Plunk your leather wallet in a tub full of water. As it slowly sinks and your valuable papers begin to disintegrate, imagine that the tub had been a lake or river that you were forced to cross late one very wet night. The point is made. So forget that experiment. A ruined wallet is all you will get for your research.

But do try this experiment: Cram a Field & Sports Wallet with as many papers as you can stow. Go ahead—shove in bills, credit cards, and the rest; it's a spacious billfold. Then toss it in the water. It will *not* sink. That's because this nylon packcloth billfold is washable, lightweight, and water repellent. And it floats.

Comfortable and form-fitting, this wallet features five internal pockets for cash, papers, pictures, and whatnot, all securely fastened with a Velcro trifold flap for extrasnug safety whether you're out on a country romp or deep into a covert mission.

Price: $7.95.

Supplier: Brigade Quartermasters.

Alco-Check

It is one of those inscrutable Chinese rituals and an interminable staple at every welcoming dinner for foreign dignitaries—which in this case means you. The Chinese host smilingly says a few words—then up and down in a quick swallow goes his shot glass. You *must* do the same. Again and again because, each in his turn, a dozen more Chinese rise, say a toast, and—drop anchor—it's down the hatch with the booze.

The room blurs. The words of praise grow dimmer. Your face reddens. Your stomach churns. You reach for another glass, because a taste of the hair of the dog that bit you may be just what you need to beat away the numbness that's spreading throughout your body and mind.

"Stop," the head of your delegation hisses in your ear. "No more tonight. You're drunk already, and you know too much—too many secrets."

It would not do, you realize, for you to become deeply inebriated, not in this arena.

But you're thirsty. You damn well want that refill. Dare you risk it?

Alco-Check takes the game out of your decision. Small enough (4 ounces and 6″ × 2½″ × 1¾″) to fit in the corner of a briefcase, it's a battery-powered drunk tester—one that matched the performance of official police breath-testing units in trials conducted by the San Francisco Police Department. Designed in Sweden, Alco-Check flashes a bright red light when your level of intoxication hits the common legal limit (0.10 percent alcohol in the bloodstream); a yellow light warns when you're nearing the danger point; and green means all systems are go. One puff of air into the mouthpiece is all it takes to get an answer fast. So let Alco-Check take the chance out of the next drink. You'll keep your secrets longer.

Price: $78.

Supplier: Sharper Image.

Healthteam

The boss laughed when he gave you the order. You both knew what it meant. "Track down Poe," he cackled. "You're to play odd man out and that's an order from the *very* top. And I do mean top," he said in his own fashion. "Tippy top—because Poe is hiding out atop Mount Everest." He laughed until he wheezed, and then left you alone to your miserable thoughts.

You stubbed your cigarette out. Mount Everest! You took the vodka jug from a desk drawer, emptied the coffee cup into the trash, and refilled it with booze. You swallowed hard. You had to *climb* Mount Everest.

That means it's time to get in shape, and soon. Good thing Healthteam is on your side. This machine will not do pushups for you. It will never run laps in your stead. But it is the first digital blood pressure/pulse monitor

that's small enough to be carried and used everywhere. Lightweight (8 ounces) and compact (5¾″ × 3½″ × 1½″), Healthteam comes with its own travel kit plus a Velcro arm cuff with built-in piezoelectric microphone and rapid-action inflator bulb. Slip the cuff on, and a few quick pumps later Healthteam flashes out the news about your blood pressure in bright fluorescent digits. Press a button and it reveals your pulse rate in beats per minute.

Healthteam operates on penlight batteries, too, so it can be used in the field—or while exercising—for instant monitoring of how your circulatory system fares.

Price: $149.

Supplier: Sharper Image.

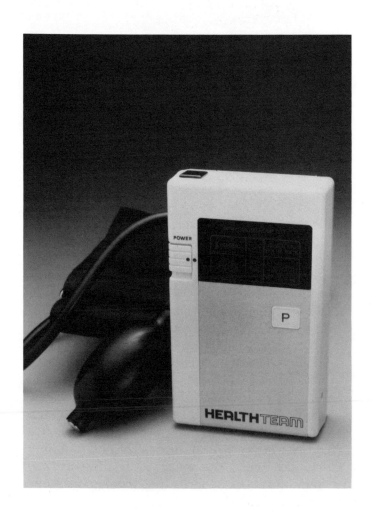

Gemini II

You know the murder weapon is buried deep in the sand at Malibu beach and the gold cache is on the bottom of Toluca Lake. Or maybe you're thinking of retiring on the thick silver vein you're convinced lies somewhere under your property. Forget the shovel—there'd be far too much digging.

Don't forget Gemini II, however. It's a professional-grade metal detector, one that scans water or land to a depth of 22 feet. Whether you're searching for a bulky .44 magnum or that Phi Beta Kappa key you lost at Aunt Florence's garden party, Gemini II is made for the job. Because if it's metal and it's

hidden, this ultrasensitive device will locate it.

Wait, you say: It's just a hobbyist's tool you want. There are answers for you as well—like Hustler II, a sensitive detector that sniffs out small objects to a 6-inch depth and can track large objects down to 3 feet. Extremely lightweight at 2½ pounds, Hustler II is not the tool for finding that gold. But it will bring you pounds of coins, lost watches, and like oddments during an afternoon scan at the local beach.

Price: $439.95 for Gemini II; Hustler II is $99.95.

Supplier: Edmund Scientic.

TravelVision

Don't be deceived by the romance. It can get boring, this surveillance work—hour after tedious hour spent sitting in a parked car, just waiting for a mark who never shows; the interminable train trips and car drives to and from safe houses—yes, all is not glamour and excitement in espionage.

But relief is a quick touch away. Just hit the On switch of Panasonic's TravelVision, and in a flash you're treated to a video smorgasbord. That's because despite its tiny, palm-size dimensions ($7\frac{1}{2}'' \times 3\frac{1}{4}'' \times 1\frac{3}{4}''$), TravelVision is a real operating television set made for true portability. Take it camping, in car pools, to sporting events (catch instant replays of the critical action). TravelVision goes everywhere, since it's battery powered (AC adapter included at no charge) and will conveniently stow in a suitcase or purse.

The screen measures $1\frac{1}{2}$ inches, but a snap-on magnifying lens will clearly blow up that image for easier, sharper viewing. And if silence is a must on your mission, a plug-in earphone comes in the package.

Price: $199.95.

Supplier: Markline.

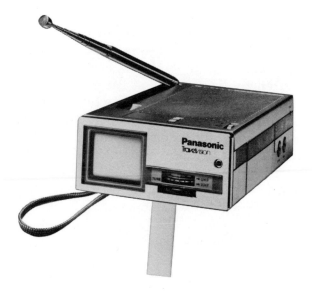

Alert U

It is an old spy trick for flushing out a suspect, and the neatness of it lies in the ready accessibility of the main but lethal ingredient. Oh, it is a touch mad, but it works. The quarry's door may be locked, bolted or barred to keep intruders at bay. But those barriers come down fast after a case-hardened spy squirts a can of lighter fluid under the door and follows up the dousing with a flaming match. Poof! There's a holocaust within— guaranteed—and *nobody* will be remaining inside.

You've heard that story, and it nags at your memory. Especially when you're traveling. You remember as well the rash of hotel/ casino fires that swept Las Vegas not long ago, and the immense body counts that resulted.

No wonder you never get a good night's sleep in a hotel bed: you're always sniffing for smoke, even in your dreams. So you awaken tired, and on missions in the field that's a gargantuan strike against you.

Pack an Alert-U and you'll sleep tight from now on. You've got smoke alarms in your home; why not in your hotel room? Alert-U is the affirmative answer to that question.

It's a palm-size portable smoke alarm that slips into odd suitcase corners. But smallness notwithstanding, it's got an extraordinary nose for the smoke that smoldering fires give off. Juse one whiff and Alert-U lets blast an extraloud alarm that's powerful enough to awaken you from the soundest dreams.

No installation is required, of course. A small clip on Alert-U's back allows it to be hung easily on any picture or door. Conventional 9-volt batteries supply the power.

For safety's sake, there's a test button that tells if all systems are go, and a battery-

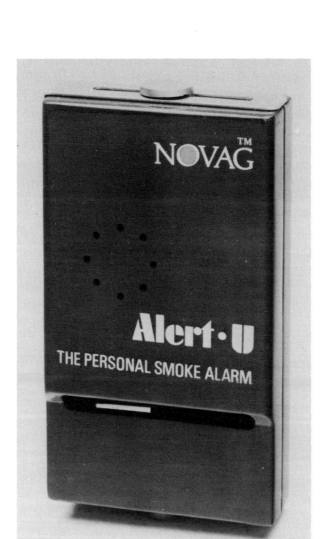

World's Finest Flashlight

It's dark. Raining. The wind howls. And you don't know what the devil is making that grunting noise outside your hideout. Which means it is time to investigate with the World's Finest Flashlight.

The claim of excellence is unyieldingly absolute. This flashlight is *the* choice of many police, firefighters, pilots, and others who need a light source that can always be depended on. The World's Finest Flashlight it is.

It's made of heavy-duty aircraft aluminum, $\frac{1}{8}$-inch thick, and is totally rust-proofed with a black anodized finish inside and out. Go ahead: Bump it; drop it; bash it; dunk it. The body will not break. And the shockproof bulb mounting protects the lens and bulb, too.

low indicator provides a fail-safe signal—all of which means that with Alert-U on your team, a hotel bed will soon become as safe as those proverbial mother's arms.

Price: $24.95.

Supplier: Western States Sales & Marketing.

Strong rubber seals keep out water, and the no-slip knurled handle provides a sure grip—just in case that grunting noise comes from someone who needs his light put out in a hurry.

Price: $28.95 for the 12¼-inch-long model.
$20.95 for the 8¼-inch-long model.

Supplier: Brookstone.

Waterproof Pocket Flashlight

The document is at the bottom of the Black Lagoon. You'd gladly fulfill the terms of your assignment; fact is, you'd be far more than glad to retrieve the papers and put an end to this tense business. But first you have to find them, and in the murky gloom of those waters, that is no mean feat.

Shed a bit of light on the matter—and on the document, too. Just reach into your pocket and pull out this tiny 5¾-inch flashlight and your problems are at an end.

Submerge most flashlights and that is that. They will shed no more light until they

dry out, and maybe not ever again. Not so with this model. It's waterproof because its supertough plastic components are hermetically sealed with an "0" ring that will keep water out to depths of 2000 feet. Operating on two conventional AA batteries (purchased separately), it puts out a potent 1400-candlepower beam through its clear polycarbonate lens—ample light to see the bottom of the Black Lagoon, prowl through abandoned offices at night, go snail hunting in the rain, or just work on a stalled car at a darkened highway's edge.

For carrying ease a lanyard may be attached through a hole at the end of the case.

Price: $10.95.

Supplier: Brookstone.

Litebox

The blackness of the night encases you. You hear the snap of a twig and it's loud enough to put you on edge, small enough to make you still more nervous. Don't let darkness be your potentially lethal enemy. Erase it utterly with a flash from the Litebox—a con-

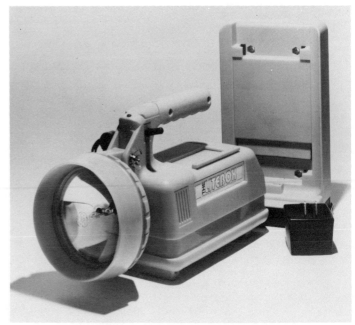

venient, portable source of continuous and powerful light.

LiteBox is ideal for use in electrical failures and on camping and boating trips as well as for security operations (it will hook up with alarm systems for automatic illumination in emergencies). It weighs just 6.1 pounds. But when fully charged, it will deliver at least 3½ hours of steady, bright light—2500 candlepower worth. It will never fail you, either, because a charge indicator is built in. A handy charging rack (which conveniently plugs into a standard wall outlet for economical power) is also provided.

Price: $119.95.

Supplier: Streamlight.

Mountain House Security Pak

The other side has finally done it. And you are just inches—minutes—away from being done in. Your guard must have slipped. No matter how it happened, you knew it was bad when you heard the ear-shattering explosion ripping through the boat. Your reflexes didn't fail you, however, and you quickly unstrapped the lifeboat and freed it from the torn, sinking yacht.

That was the good news. The bad news is that you're hundreds of miles from the nearest land, and already the sharks are hungrily circling your flimsy raft. Wait—is that another boat you hear off in the distance? Save your breath. There's no screaming loud enough; nobody will ever notice.

But don't give up. Remember, you're a professional and you thrive on life-and-death dilemmas. Plus you've taken to heart the Boy Scout motto: Be prepared. So you are.

Look in that corner cubbyhole. There's the Security Pak you stowed. And inside is your life—at least that's what the Security Pak can deliver when the situation is extreme, like this one. Because in it are flares, waterproof matches, first-aid essentials, a whistle, and a signal mirror. You're equipped for SOS signals galore. But if they're ignored, you've also got a supply of solid fuel tablets, a plastic tube tent, a razor blade, nylon cord, and duct tape. You won't starve, either, since there's an assortment of freeze-dried foods totaling seven complete meals (with menus like beef and rice, and orangeade to drink). Add up the contents of this lightweight (7.25 pounds) emergency pack and it provides the ingredients to keep you afloat and alive for several days or longer if it comes down to that.

Suspicious about those freeze-dried foods? Edibility and freshness are guaranteed for years, and—the manufacturer promises—the dehydrated morsels contain all the nutrients and vitamins of fresh food. There's no disputing taste, however, and you can inexpensively gauge how *your* taste reacts to these goodies by dining on the Sampler Pak: Eleven freeze-dried foods including entrées (beef Stroganoff), appetizers (shrimp with cocktail sauce), vegetables (peas), and fruits (peaches).

Not for spies and unlucky sailors alone, freeze-dried foods are much coveted by campers, survivalists, Mormons, and eschatologists. Anybody, that is, who's prepared for a rainy day and worse.

Prices: Security Pak With Survival Items— $73.00.
Sampler Pack—$26.70.

Supplier: The Larder—Survival Books.

SPACE AGE EXOTICA

IF YOU SAW IT IN A JAMES BOND MOVIE, *no matter how exotic and outlandish the device was, it is now on the espionage marketplace or soon will be. Nothing, it seems, is beyond the grasp of the imaginations of the technical wizards who create the tools of espionage.*

A classic case in point is that for decades spies scoffed at the available tools for silencing a firearm's fatal bang-bang. Every device on the market ruined a marksman's aim and sharply decreased what is politely known as the "penetrating power" of fired rounds. So silencers, except in the most delicate circumstances, were eschewed by professionals. Until *Mitch WerBell, a flamboyant gunrunner and entrepreneur (his business ventures have included Cobra, a camp for teaching corporate bodyguards to be killers) designed his "suppressor": a silencer that not only eliminated sound but improved the accuracy and the stopping power of the gun. They said it couldn't be done, but thanks to Col. Mitch, spies can now blow each other's heads off, not with a bang but a whimper.*

In many quarters you will also hear that it is impossible to detect a tape recorder. Nonsense. It's true enough that until recently tape-recorder detectors were junk. But no longer. Newly marketed detectors key into tape recorders' bias oscillators—a common sound-enhancing component—and that's a sure way to sniff out the presence of a concealed recorder. Except not always. New espionage recorders feature a lead shield to muffle the oscillation or, in some instances, simply delete that component. And second-generation detectors, you can bet, will zero in on yet another component.

Computer companies, on the other hand, still live in unabated and continuing fear of tape recorders. The two technologies appear unconnected? True. But computers do produce an audible and potentially meaningful tat-tat-tat as they process and print out their data. Record those noises and analyze them and you're on top of the other side's secrets. As a result, many computers now feature sophisticated baffles and sound deadeners to thwart eavesdroppers. Yet there is no known instance of this manner of computer theft.

Getting the impression you are on a not-so-merry merry-go-round? This technological trench warfare is ceaseless. An espionage boutique, for instance, recently unveiled its antikidnap gadgetry line in which the highest-tech centerpiece is a tiny transmitter that can be implanted surgically in dental work and will escape detection by the other side because it's guaranteed to remain dead until a paired homing device goes on a frantic search for it. When the search begins, the transmitter pops into liveliness, and the victim, says the boutique, can be traced to within five feet of his or her location, no matter how far away that is. Sound too bizarre to be true? Does the device exist? Are US diplomats and top agents sporting it, as the manufacturer claims?

The answers, sadly, are unknown. There is a Zen rub at work throughout the espionage community: All such questions go forever unanswered. One side will publicly laugh at another's technological claims—while all the time knowing those claims are true. Another side will assert that it has birthed a technological revolution when it hasn't. But nobody will issue a denial. Insiders are absorbed by these moves and countermoves; that's their purpose. Outsiders, in the process, are baffled.

Yet this much is certain: Space-age espionage gadgets do exist, and they are for sale to the public. At least a handful are, and that's this chapter's core.

SAT Briefcase

You've spent ten years of your life compiling the goods on the baddies of Hollywood and their underworldly dealings. It's time to deliver your report. But the word is out, and you know the folks at the studios are just dying to get their hands on your reams of revealing facts. So, of course, you tote the report in the SAT briefcase. It looks innocuous, ordinary—but just let some thug of an alleged producer touch it, and first an alarm blares noisily and then a conspicuous cloud of red smoke billows into the air. Red dye will stain the contents of SAT, too, so if Mr. Sleazo or his pinkie ring–wearing buddies do manage to make off with SAT, you can always catch them literally red-handed later. Truth is, however, it's unlikely that the Tinsel Gang would get that far, because SAT's built-in safe defies entry by cutting, breaking, burning, and almost all other means. For more thorough security, SAT's alarm and smoke-dye systems are operated by one key; a second key is required to open the safe, and that key may be stowed elsewhere for secure keeping.

So hand in that report, and who knows, maybe next year there will be furious bidding for the movie rights.

Price: $1325.

Supplier: The Rouse Company.

Trionic Briefcase

Once you're outfitted with all the tools of the spy trade, how do you lug this mountain about? Not in a shopping bag, that's for sure. Try the 008 Trionic Briefcase instead.

Disguised as a nondescript attaché case, the Trionic Briefcase's innards give the lie to its unimposing exterior. Steal it, for instance, and an earsplitting howl erupts from within and alerts all in hearing range to this attempted thievery. Worried about armed assailants? Not if you tote the Trionic Briefcase: Its ordinary-appearing outside doubles as a bullet-proof shield. Bugging and related eavesdropping stunts are your concern? The Trionic Briefcase comes equipped with a tiny light that warns of the presence of listening devices.

Add it up and the Trionic Briefcase is the dream present on every spy's wish list. No matter what gadget is wanted—from devices to detect explosive vapors through petite tape recorders, disabling light guns, and tracking transmitters in the event you are abducted—the Trionic Briefcase affords a stylishly commodious home. If there is a *ne plus ultra* in avocational espionage gear, the Trionic Briefcase wins the laurels.

Price: $770 and up. (For $770 the buyer gets the briefcase and bullet-proof shield, antitheft alarm, and Security Blanket light flasher. Other items are optional extras, and the outfit's cost can soar to $6000 and well beyond, depending upon the tastes and bankroll of the purchaser.)

Supplier: CCS.

CEB 1000

Espionage hardware is shocking—sometimes quite literally so. CEB 1000 is painful proof. Disguised as an ordinary briefcase, it's a foolproof theft deterrent for any courier of sensitive papers or valuables. That's because it *is* a briefcase—one commodious enough to hold reams of secrets—but it's got another, more alert and meaner side.

The wariness comes with the homing device the courier wears on his body. Whenever courier and case are close to each other, all's well. Separate them by 15 feet, however, and the homing gadget tells the courier he's strayed. A prealert beep signals that message, and that gives the courier several seconds to press the button that tells CEB 1000 that everything's A-Okay. If everything is *not* fine—if, for instance, CEB 1000's been snatched—the courier now need only ignore the beep. And CEB 1000 turns downright angry. The first sign is a prompt and continuous blast from the built-in alarm siren. Then, for good measure, a jarring 2000 volts of electricity soar through CEB 1000—and that's juice enough to addle any would-be thief.

Price: $1195.

Supplier: Ted L. Gunderson & Associates.

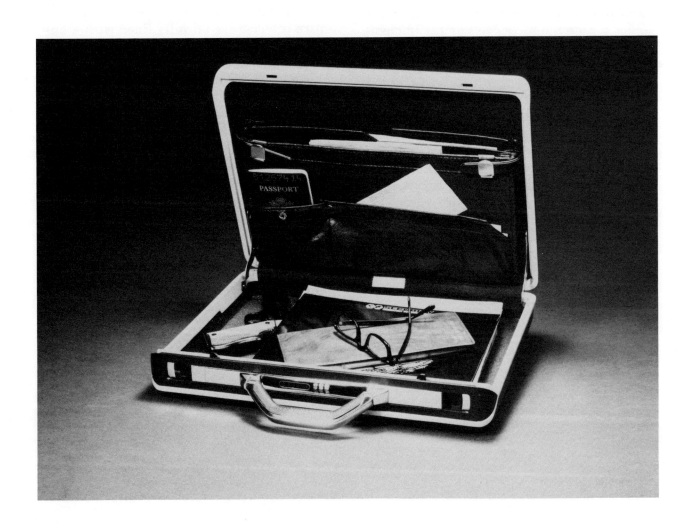

Vehicle Following System

"Follow that car," you bellow at your driver. And you relax. This pursuit is a cakewalk, and you know you'll not be thrown off course by hairpin turns, manic acceleration, or any of the rest of the *Bullitt* stunts. That's because you are not relying on driving skills alone: The 1012 Vehicle Follower System is on your side.

Good for tracking people and parcels as well as vehicles, the system includes a battery-operated receiver, relative direction meter, magnetic mount transmitter, and beacon transmitter. But the compact beacon is the key. Small and with self-contained batteries, the beacon is quickly concealed on the target (under a car's bumpers, say) and it immediately gets busy sending out its regular, trackable signals. The receiver, in turn, picks up the signals and allows you to pinpoint the subject's location precisely at distances of up to ten miles. (As with all low-power radios, transmission distance varies with terrain and weather. On a stormy day amid midtown Manhattan's skyscrapers or in a blizzard in the Rocky Mountains, for instance, expect a range considerably shorter than 10 miles.)

A bonus with this system is that the receiver is mobile and portable, so it can be deployed in a car, a helicopter, a boat, or an office. And it features three-channel capability to enable you to track three beacons simultaneously.

Your target, in any case, can remain blissfully oblivious to the goings-on, since the beacon itself is tiny and its signal is essentially inaudible. On the other hand, for defensive purposes you may opt to tote the beacon yourself so *your* side will always know your whereabouts on delicate, sensitive missions.

Price: $3695.
Supplier: LEA.

Supercar

It was good enough for the Shah of Iran during the last, violent days of his troubled regime. He saw one and instantly knew that, even more than his secret Savak police, this would keep him safe from howling mobs and desperate assassination attempts. That's why the Shah put in a rush order for the invincible Supercar, a fortress on wheels—it's an automobile that cannot be stopped by bullets, bombs, or terrorist attacks.

Start out with a Bentley or a VW Bug. The choice is yours. But no matter the base vehicle, in all windows you'll have bullet-proof glass strong enough to withstand a blast from a .30-caliber carbine, and tough enough to deflect smashes from rocks, boots, and hatchets. The gas tank, battery, and entire interior are all fully lined with a bullet-proof fabric that's both stronger and lighter than steel. The car's bottom is coated to withstand the impact of land-mine or grenade explosions. And the tires are bolstered with steel so they will not deflate even when shot point-blank.

That's a taste of your defenses in Supercar. You're also ready to fight back. If the other side tries to run you off the road, ram them with your steel-reinforced bumpers. Or hit a button and shoot out thirty gallons of slick diesel fuel to send the enemy slithering wildly off course. Spray tear gas at angry mobs through Supercar's ducts, or use the flip-down gun portholes in the car's doors for those times when they just won't take "no" for an answer.

There's a traitor in your midst? Sit him down on the front seat next to the driver's. Hit the control and *Bamm!* you've detonated the trio of loaded shotgun shells that are positioned under that seat for dependable disposal of unwanted guests.

Fully equipped, Supercar's package also includes a Bomb Spy that detects vapors of any kind and lets you know if explosives are nearby; easily activated tracking transmit-

ters so you can be located in case of kidnapping or abduction; emergency oxygen tanks to keep you breathing in smoke or gas; and infrared goggles for clear-sighted vision in total darkness, smoke, and fog.

To help you stay in touch with your side, there are video scanners for HQ to keep you in sight and a UHF-VHF system with a built-in scrambler to keep you in tap-free hearing range. There are, as well, built-in devices to guard against breakins, bugs, and all manner of recording gadgets.

And just in case someone does defy the odds and manages to wire your car to explode when the key is turned, there's a remote-controlled ignition for safe starting at a distance.

Thorough as this transformation is, it takes but 30 days and adds surprisingly little weight to what was once an ordinary car . . . and still looks just like one.

Incidentally, for the curious, the Shah's fall was in no way connected to Supercar. He lost the throne before taking delivery.

Price: $100,000–$250,000 (exact cost depends upon specific options selected. A kit for bullet-proofing any car is available independent of Supercar. It comes in various levels of thoroughness to meet your precise needs and can be installed readily by any car owner to keep its presence confidential.)

Supplier: CCS.

LOOKING BEYOND THE LOOKING GLASS: MORE RESOURCES

SPYING IS A FAST-TRACK PROFESSION. *Russia's new head of state, Yuri Andropov, is a former KGB spymaster. To those who think a spymaster couldn't make it to the top in the United States, think again. The proverbial heartbeat away is a former top dog for the CIA, George Bush. Spies get the very best dirt, and to the most dextrous diggers, promotions come fast.*

Digging good dirt isn't easy, however. It takes training. And retraining. At the CIA, for instance, the opening educational salvo is a several-month-long stint at "The Farm," and refresher courses are scheduled whenever assignments require additional knowledge. While spies do specialize—some excel at "wet jobs," some are buggers, some are couriers, and more are analysts—any spy who goes out into the field without an intimate familiarity with most aspects of the business is sure to become "the late spy" soon.

Steady advances in technology make continual training necessary. Just when you've mastered administering (or defeating) polygraph lie detectors, that device is put on the shelf and voice-stress analyzers become à la mode. Learn VSAs and, depend on it, a newer-fangled gadget will sweep the espionage community. That's why education—and highly specialized technical assistance from consultants who devote their lives to keeping abreast of the field of spying and its component niches—is indispensable. And obtainable through the additional sources listed in the pages that follow.

Professional Countermeasures Sweeps

It is an impromptu meeting, but a crucially sensitive one. You're talking with a top agent from the other side at last, and he says the subject on his mind is defecting. Reel in this fish and it's an unparalleled coup. Lose him and if word were ever to leak out, it'd be an unprecedented and disgraceful blot on your record. Consequently you must proceed with the utmost discretion and the most extreme secrecy. Neither your team nor his side can suspect that this meeting took place; only catastrophe could result.

But, damn, you've so little time to prepare. Your home is out; that's obvious. So is the office. It must be neutral turf, like a hotel room. But it must be turf that is secure and wholly free of bugs, taps, any eavesdropping devices. Your career rests on this.

You could do the exterminating yourself, but you're a spy, an espionage agent, *not* an expert debugger. And this definitely is a case where a professional is required.

Call in Ted L. Gunderson & Associates. A member of the Society of Former Special Agents of the Federal Bureau of Investigation, Gunderson specializes in providing thorough countermeasures sweeps, as they are called in this trade, and these sweeps are aimed squarely at rooting out and destroying all manner of bugs and pests, including ones usually reserved for top-drawer national-security applications.

Bring Gunderson and his gang in on the job and, in a Class A Sweep, a computer-assisted spectrum analyzer will be unleashed to find sophisticated microwave bugs, infra-red transmitters, radio-type devices, and suspiciously loose wires. A skilled physical search of the premises finishes the job. And if there's an unwanted bug aboard, these detailed precautions will kill it surer than DDT.

If it's not a room that concerns you but your telephone, call Gunderson in on that, too. After his array of high-tech gadgets analyze resistance, inductance, capacitance, system voltage, and current, you'll get a fast and sure yea or nay verdict.

A yea comes back on both the room sweep and the telephone check, and it's clear you've got bugs? Solutions are yours—not Gunderson's—to devise. But you are the spy. And the police are just a quick call away.

Prices: Class A Room Sweep—$1.75 per square foot ($500 minimum).
Single Line Telephone Check—$150.00. (Air-travel time is an additional $20/hour plus expenses.)
Note: Class B and Class C Room Sweeps, involving less deployment of gadgetry by the antibug squad, cost $.75 and $.50 per square foot, respectively.

Supplier: Ted L. Gunderson & Associates.

Countermeasures Training

You move fast. But the other side, it sometimes seems, moves faster. Just when you install a sophisticated bug detector, the other side changes gears and employs still newer high-tech devices that effectively and mockingly sidestep every countermeasure you've taken. When you finally bow to brutal reality and buy a bullet-proof vest, the other side junks its .357 magnums in favor of hand-held rocket launchers. A pessimistic picture? Admittedly. But not a wholly false one.

Ten years ago no home had a computer. Ten years from now most homes will. Mull on that revolution and understand this: Much the same technological genius is currently at work in espionage circles, with the same dramatic consequences.

Consider the inspired work of the legendary Bernie Spindel, for instance. Trained as a wireman by the Army Signal Corps during World War II, Spindel applied for a job at the CIA at war's end. He was rejected, but, undaunted, he started his own private investigation firm. And he proceeded to overturn the state of the art of surveillance. One Spindel insight is that it is not difficult—in fact, it is simple—to use advanced laser technology to bug conversations in a room by standing outside and "reading" the sound vibrations recorded on the windowpanes. Or if a more detailed record is desired, additional lasers can be employed to record pictures of whatever is going on in that room—all done without anybody inside ever suspecting a tap is at work.

That is just the tip of the Spindel iceberg. Another Spindel invention, one he had yet to perfect at his death, has its roots in the recognition that common water is an extraordinary conductor of sound. With this in mind, Spindel decided—and no scientist would disagree—that in theory a bug could be concealed in a building's plumbing, where it would be unlikely to be detected. With that device and the conducting properties of water working in harness, a conversation could be clearly "overheard" miles away. Science fiction? Not at all. Spindel had advanced to the point where all he needed to pull that stunt off was equipment capable of filtering out the cacophony of unwanted noises, and then he could have flushed a bug down a White House toilet, say, and bugged the whole place from the Madison Hotel a mile removed from the executive mansion. No, Spindel did not finish this project. But he died over a decade ago, in 1971, and nobody knows if another surveillance visionary came along to complete the design. But the smart money says that his system or one of equal revolutionary magnitude is now at work.

Is surrender to this high-tech wave of snooping the only option? Embrace ignorance and the answer is yes. Keep abreast of the technological developments, however, and no matter what the other side unleashes, you'll be ready. Knowledge, in this instance, is indisputably power, because you'll know their best tricks as soon as they do. And that's your edge in preparing . . . and fighting back.

How to get—and keep—that sharp edge? Enroll in Information Security Associates Countermeasures Training Seminar. It's a thorough, in-depth, eight-hour course that will give you the lowdown—the *lowest* lowdown—on the newest in clandestine methodologies, technologies, and attack stratagems. You'll be updated on the equipment necessary to fight back, from bug detectors through telephone analyzers, and shown exactly where and how to put that equipment to best use.

Training is by professionals, and in every instance the course is crafted to meet the individual's needs. Although instruction is available at your home or office or at ISA's Stamford, Connecticut, headquarters, ISA strongly recommends your place for best tailoring of the program to your specific wants and espionage problems.

Price: $400 (for training at ISA's HQ).

$300 (for training at your place; travel expenses are extra).

(NOTE: The tuition fee is a flat charge. Any number of persons may attend; the rate remains unchanged. But ISA recommends a maximum enrollment of four for best results.)

Supplier: Information Security Associates.

Rouse School of Private Investigation

This is one case you wish would fade away. The specter of defeat haunts you. Dozens of times you've seen your target. You know her face—every pore, the small semicircular scar below her right nostril. And well do you know her smile.

You're certain she is selling secrets, the most sensitive sorts, to the other side. But she is slick, too slick. She's eluded your every snare, mocked all your tricks and traps. And still she meets with the other side. You know now that you cannot catch her red-handed. Face it: Your skills, good as they are, are outclassed.

But don't drop your calling. Upgrade your skills—with a thorough correspondence course of study of the methods, modes, and techniques of the contemporary private investigator. You'll work through the lessons at your own pace, in your home. But your progress will be continually, closely monitored by a professional investigator/instructor whose job it is to pass on the latest in investigative techniques and the craft of espionage.

The course is not just theory. Every lesson is alive with vivid, graphic, true-to-life encounters, all designed to give you that edge of preparedness when you operate against the other side in the field.

Which field practices will you master? Complete the Rouse course of private investigation and you'll be fully fluent in antiterrorist tactics; Spiderman-like techniques for scaling skyscrapers; industrial espionage; electronic eavesdropping; high-speed pursuit; locks and lock picking; and reconnaissance, surveillance, and undercover techniques. Plus you'll study an array of more conventional tactics like fingerprinting, witness interrogation, and how to locate missing persons.

But investigation increasingly is a high-tech venture, and the Rouse School recognizes that, too. Its Advanced Course is devoted to a detailed probe of the most sophisticated wrinkles in investigative electronics—precisely the sort of tools found through this catalog. So if you're puzzled by how best to use Rearoscope surveillance glasses or mystified by the intricacies of your telephone line analyzer, the Rouse School will fill you in and make you that much more effective where it counts—in the field.

The basic course of study consists of twenty lessons. The Advanced Course adds fifteen more. Diplomas are granted to graduates, and the Rouse School is provisionally approved by the California State Department of Public Instruction. Enrollment is open only to applicants with no felony convictions.

Prices: Basic Course—$195.
Advanced Course—$340.

Supplier: Rouse School of Detective Training.

The Custom Knife

Do it yourself if you want it done right. It's a rule that applies in life, which means it applies all the more in espionage, where life is not just another four-letter word. Because in spying, the arrival of your next breath is never a given. Not when one tiny wrong move could spell your doom. And so could the wrong knife.

Why a knife? It's the basic field survival tool. It will kill, but in a pinch it will also double as a saw, a shovel, table cutlery, a surgical instrument, a shaver. Add it up and a good knife is a spy's most versatile and indispensable tool. That's why you need the very best.

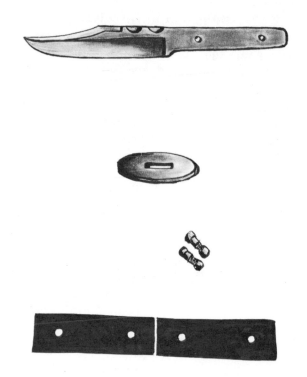

dependably, ruggedly hard but enormously flexible. A Morseth will bend to a 45-degree angle without breaking.

Choose a handle now; stag, from India, is the top of the line. Extraordinarily dense, Schrimsher's stag is made to absorb abuse.

Odds and ends are all that remain: a fitting to hold the two handle pieces together and attached to the blade; maybe pearl scales to add a stylish tone; a few screws, some washerlike spacers (to keep the blade more firmly in place), and you've done it—the Custom Knife is built.

Intrigued but bewildered? Study *How Knives Are Made,* a thorough primer on the craft. Or, to get a surer feel before plunging into full customizing, buy a boot-knife kit. Provided in the kit are all the required parts, and assembly is elementary.

Prices: Morseth Blade—$35.00–$50.00 (depending on size).
Stag Handles—$5.00–$8.00 per pair.
Pearl Scales—$8.00 per pair.
Fittings—$2.50–$3.50.
How Knives Are Made—$15.00.
Boot Knife Kit—$29.95.

(NOTE: Knives to meet *any* need can be constructed out of Schrimsher's raw materials. Prices vary widely, contingent on exact pieces selected, but typical prices for a complete knife vary from $25–$100.)

Supplier: The Custom Knife.

Make your own and you'll know you've got it. Especially if you take your lead from the Custom Knifemaker, Bob Schrimsher. Schrimsher does not make knives, although he is available for consultation. What he does instead is sell the quality parts needed for assembly of knives.

Custom knifemaking is not akin to do-it-yourself brain surgery. To get started all that's needed are the raw ingredients . . . plus a chunk of time. The pieces—in particular, the blade—are indeed raw, and considerable time must be devoted to honing, sharpening, polishing. Blade aside, however, the rest of the job is largely a matter of swiftly putting together a few parts and tightening a few screws. You've got the time? Good: Your investment will yield you a superlative knife at the best price around.

Start with the blade, and pick the best, a Morseth. Made of Norwegian steel, these blades come in an array of shapes and lengths from 3½ inches to 7 inches and are

K-9 Command Dogs

Beware of Dog. That's what the bright red sign with white lettering proclaims. Heinz snorts when he sees it. With the Albanian plans in your home, a little *caveat* on the front door is not going to deter the East German agent from his work. He glances at his watch, and he knows that in just five minutes the papers will be his. You will be dead.

He is not subtle; that has never been Heinz's hallmark. He slams the sledgehammer through the living-room window and grunts, "Hold on, I'm coming." In Heinz comes.

There is the slightest sound, not unlike denim ripping in strong hands. A dark blur. Then a pained scream that does not cease until you sharply speak. "Heel, Beelzelbub."

The dog halts. Heinz remains still. Not even Heniz will dare move again; not with that monster of a dog, his menacingly sharp teeth bared, hovering over him. Mark up another vicotry for a well trained guard dog.

Guns will stop a well schooled dog. Little else will. Persistence, dedication, and a tough faithfulness are a guard dog's style. But there is a world of difference between a playful pooch and a guard dog; never forget that. Definitely the guard dog can and will be friendly to you and those you designate, but not to anyone else. Others he will lunge into with abandon, because that is his history and his destiny. Make no mistake, however; few dogs possess the raw talents necessary to be a superlative guard dog, just as few people have the basic skills required to be a top-notch spy.

Trainer Jack Healy knows which dogs have the stuff. That's his business, and he is world-recognized as among the very best. You've got a dog you want trained? Ask Jack. He'll put Rover through preliminary paces and, if the dog earns passing grades, enroll him in a rigorous training program, out of which will come a friendly, affectionate, but deadly-when-commanded beast, one that can be counted on to provide around-the-clock protection and surveillance of any area you mark as his to watch. Burglars, intruders, vandals—all will be given a quick, furry welcome. And they'll make a quicker exit, most likely minus a patch or two of flesh. They will *not* be killed, since the dog's assignment is simply to chase away uninvited guests. But they *will* be chased away; depend on it.

Maybe you have specialized needs? Like bomb detection, narcotics searches, rescue and training work? Healy's schooling covers those assignments on request.

Want the best, the most reliable protection? Start from scratch and begin the regimen with a puppy bought directly from Healy's kennels. Do that and you're assured that the dog has been bred and selected for temperament, tenacity, toughness, and intelligence. It's a dog that's not vicious but is a specialist. Just like any other agent. Except, with the dog, there's a huge plus. There are many, many fewer canine defectors.

Prices: German Shepherd Puppy—$950. Doberman Puppy—$1250.

(NOTE: Training, which begins at six months and is tailored to meet individual needs, is additional. Costs vary with the program selected and average $1000–$5000.)

Supplier: K-9 Command Dogs.

The Central Intelligence Agency

So you want to be a real-life spy? Go to the source: the CIA.

Every major nation has a bustling intelligence group—or, less euphemistically, spy shop—and in the United States, the lead organization is the Central Intelligence Agency. The mammoth but supersecret National Security Agency, which is largely concerned with intercepting all manner of international radio transmissions and devising codes to break into enemy transmissions, and the Pentagon's Defense Intelligence Agency are two others.

In the Soviet Union, the KGB and the GRU (the less well known military intelligence operation) are the CIA's counterparts. In Israel it's the Mossad, a shop that takes secrecy so seriously that a former head received his walking papers because he was identified in a domestic newspaper. MI-6 does the espionage for England. In France it's the *Service de Documentation Exterieure et de Contre-Espionage* (SDECE). Scrutinize every nation of international importance as well as those which aspire to that status, and you're sure to find a homespun intelligence apparatus somewhere in the bowels of each government.

Real-life spying, however, unlike the Walter Mitty variety, does have a few drawbacks. For one thing, you can't trust *anybody*. After all, if you go around poisoning, maiming, eavesdropping, and blackmailing, it only stands to reason that others will do the same to you . . . and to your friends . . . and your family. No big deal, you say? Well, how about this: Real-life spying is BORING. Yep, boring. And that fact leads to a peculiar paradox in the operations of the CIA in particular. While it remains shrouded in murky secrecy (medals for distinguished service, for example, are awarded in *private* Agency ceremonies . . . and promptly taken away from the recipient for safe and secret storage), the CIA nonetheless frequently runs recruitment advertisements in newspapers nationwide. It's not so much the danger that keeps the CIA's job turnover high, but boredom.

The CIA covets specialists rather than gunslingers (it boasts of employing more Ph.D.'s than any other federal agency). The Agency's chief thrust is *not* covert operations but rather overt information gathering (most CIA data is culled from close readings of *public* trade and general publications) and analysis. Computer whizzes and linguists are much in demand; assassins and dirty tricksters, while at the pinnacle of the CIA's status totem, are less intensely recruited. Want to find out for yourself? Write to the CIA and you'll be swamped by brochures and pamphlets with titles like *Intelligence: The Acme of Skill.* These, mind you, are sanitized versions of the CIA's operations. You will not be told about the assassinations of Congo leader Patrice Lumumba, Dominican Republic President Rafael Trujillo, Latin American leftist Ernesto Guevara, and the Chilean president Salvador Allende. At least the price is right, however: CIA brochures are free.

On the other hand, if you'd rather skip the CIA's squeaky-clean version of history and dive instead into the tales the Agency and the rest of the government would rather keep untold, contact Covert Action, a group founded by renegade CIA agent Philip Agee, among others. Five or so times yearly, Covert Action publishes its *Information Bulletin,* and, believe it, the CIA takes those pages very, very seriously. Read Covert Action's exposes on biochemical warfare, clandestine U.S. support for anti-Castro terrorists, fresh looks at what is going on in El Salvador, and you will understand why.

Prices: CIA pamphlets, $0; Covert Action's Information Bulletin, $15 for six issues.

Suppliers: Central Intelligence Agency. Covert Action.

WHITHER GADGETRY?

GADGETRY WILL EVOLVE: ESPIONAGE WILL GROW *more
all-encompassing, more entangled with the lives of us all. Those
are predictions, but they are sure ones. The Orwellian 1984 has long
since arrived. Computers, satellite communications, two-way
televisions, infinity transmitters, microwaves, lasers: much has
happened since US Secretary of State Henry Stimson said in 1929
that "gentlemen do not read each other's mail." Perhaps gentlemen
do not; spies do—and that is just for openers.*

*In 1970, for instance, the Federal Bureau of Investigation (an
agency that has intercepted hundreds of thousands of Americans'
mail and covertly read billions of words along the way) became
irked at a white woman who was involved in ACTION, a biracial
civil rights group. Off went the following letter to the woman's
husband: "Look, man, I guess your old lady don't get enough at
home or she wouldn't be shucking and jiving with our black men in
ACTION, you dig? Like all she wants to intergrate [sic] is the
bedroom and us Black Sisters ain't gonna take no second best from
our men. So, lay it on her man. . . ." The author? The missive was
signed "Black Sisters." It was written by the FBI. The woman and
her husband separated soon afterward.*

*If effectiveness is the yardstick, the FBI's stunt had its merits:
The women's activities in ACTION slumped; she ceased to be a
burr, real or imagined, under the bureau's saddle. All accomplished
without the use of any technology more sophisticated than a
ball-point pen.*

*Never dismiss the human element in espionage. A curious case
in point: Was the Watergate break-in bungled? An odd question,
perhaps, because on its face the Nixonian Hunt-Liddy team was the*

gang that plainly could not steal straight. Yet the spookiest of the spooks read the story differently. Note the absurdities, they say. Like the placing of tape over a door lock and, after that tape was removed by a patrolling guard who inexplicably investigated no further, the replacing of the tape in the very same spot—even though it was known that the Watergate guard adhered to a set route and would soon return. Replace the tape, these spooks point out, and you have unmistakably red-flagged your shenanigans. Incredible stupidity on the Plumbers' parts? Or a conscious, purposive undermining of the job in order to blow the lid off the Nixon administration? Hmm, hot spies sagely nod. Hmm.

Consider the CIA, the most fabled spy shop in the nation and one with a bottomless Santa's bag of technology at its disposal. What was the CIA's most storied program during the Vietnam war? A simple, nontechnical assassination business named Operation Phoenix, in which the agency identified Vietcong sympathizers in South Vietnamese hamlets and "neutralized" them.

Spy vs. spy. That, despite the technological gloss, is the espionage industry leitmotif. CIA spooks know this, and they revel in their stories: of the time a CIA team rigged a Monte Carlo casino bathroom and covertly pilfered samples of Egyptian King Farouk's urine in order to determine the monarch's health; of another time when the CIA's elite "bag boys"—agents whose specialty is illegal breaking and entering—managed to steal quietly from under the Russians' noses the original Sputnik satellite and return it safely three hours later; of the still more playful dirty tricks . . . such as the Saigon capers of the early 1960s, before the war turned meaner. Early on, for instance, the CIA grew vexed with the incompetence of South Vietnamese Premier Hoang, and that dissatisfaction was shared by native leaders who wanted to topple the Hoang government. No could do, however; not with the crack Vietnamese air force Skyraiders squadron remaining loyal to Hoang. But a CIA superspook knew the solution: One day he visited the Skyraiders' commissary and dumped pounds of laxatives in their food. Toilet-bound, the air force never rose to intervene in the coup.

This thirst for the visceral runs through much of the CIA's work in the young days of the Vietnam era. Mull on this problem: During 1964, anti-American demonstrations by Buddhist monks in Saigon were severely damaging Washington's credibility in its claims of broad-based popular backing. Question: how to stop the Buddhists? CIA answer: exploit human predilections by salting the clouds above Saigon with silver iodide and thus provoke a rainfall to dampen the Buddhists' enthusiasm for mass outdoor rallies. What happens when nature refused to cooperate with this chemical boost? Because the Buddhists wore loose garments and no underwear, the CIA recognized the opening. Whenever it remained dry and the Buddhists began a march, CIA agents infiltrated the demonstrating crowds and liberally dropped egg-size itching-powder bombs. Crunch, crunch went the capsules under the Buddhist feet; the powders flew everywhere and, in particular, upward. Exit the Buddhists, fast and scratching.

Immoral, all of this? Not in the minds of real-life spies. Though some feign a noble purpose, espionage is ultimately an amoral game. There are sides, of course, but every game requires sides. In the spy's world, the sides are arbitrary. Allegiances are made and broken on whims. Sworn vows are repudiated whenever expedient. The history of the most notorious spymaster of them all clearly shows this. During World War II General Reinhard Gehlen ran the Hitler spy network throughout Eastern Europe, and he did so with a cold, masterful skill. After the fall of the Third Reich? No visits to Nuremberg or stays in Spandau prison for Gehlen. Not even a rapid exit to Argentina. Nope; the Allies, commitments to prosecute Nazi leaders notwithstanding, promptly set Gehlen up as the new head of the West German Federal Intelligence Service: It was expedient to do so. *Gehlen already had hundreds of proven agents in place throughout the Russian zones of Europe; the Allies had nobody there . . . until Gehlen joined that side and provided an eye on Moscow's doings. Was the Allies' decision moral? Immoral? In the world of espionage the question is absurd. Effectiveness is all that matters. Gehlen's side had ceased to exist, and by joining the Allies, Gehlen enhanced their efforts against the* new *other side. He was an indispensable man.*

Espionage equipment is never indispensable. New, improved tools enter the marketplace; old gear vanishes. But an old spy—and an old spy is an effective one—just puts on a new coat. Nobody asks what color the last one was. So it goes in spydom.

MEET THE MAKERS: LEADING MANUFACTURERS AND SUPPLIERS

YOU'VE GOT A QUESTION ABOUT A PRODUCT *or two that you've read about in* The Complete Spy? *Or perhaps you're keen to make a purchase? This chapter saves you a search. Certainly not all manufacturers and by no means all suppliers and retailers of espionage equipment are featured in* The Complete Spy. *Among the more notable omissions, for instance, are a few boutiques specializing in the highest tech gear; their technology is at the sharpest cutting edge of the state of this art, and it tends to be made available only to credentialed spooks. Also absent are companies that sell* only *to federal and law-enforcement agencies. All the companies mentioned here welcome business and inquiries from the general public.*

Alcone Co.
575 Eighth Ave.
New York, NY 10018

AMC Sales
P.O. Box 928
Downey, CA 90241

Ankler Designs
P.O. Box 5636
San Juan, Puerto Rico 00905

Asian World of Martial Arts
932 Arch St.
Philadelphia, PA 19107

ASP
P.O. Box 18595
Atlanta, GA 30326

Assault Systems
826 Horan Dr.
St. Louis, MO 63026

Auto-Ordnance Corp.
West Hurley, NY 12491

Bali Song Inc.
3039 Roswell St.
Los Angeles, CA 90065

Belsaw Institute
6301 Equitable Road
P.O. Box 593
Kansas City, MO 64141

Bianchi Gunleather
100 Calle Cortez
Temecula, CA 92390

BMF Activator
P.O. Box 12364
Houston, TX 77017

Brigade Quartermasters
266 Roswell St.
Marietta, GA 30060

Brookstone
639 Vose Farm Road
Peterborough, NH 03458

Central Intelligence Agency
(CIA)
Washington, D.C. 20505

CCS (Communication Control, Inc.)
633 Third Ave.
New York, NY 10017

CFI Camera Division
100 Portland Ave.
Bergenfield, NJ 07621

Cincinnati Microwave
255 Northland Bl.
Cincinnati, OH 45246

Cose Technology Corp.
15 East 40th St.
New York, NY 10016

Covert Action
P.O. Box 50272
Washington, D.C. 20004

The Custom Knife
Custom Knifemaker's Supply
P.O. Box 308
Emory, TX 75440

Dolan's Sports
P.O. Box 26
Hwy 547
Farmingdale, NJ 07727

Edmund Scientific
101 East Gloucester Pike
Barrington, NJ 08007

Forever Safe
1126 W. Evans
Visalia, CA 93277

Goldberg's Marine
202 Market St.
Philadelphia, PA 19106

Ted L. Gunderson & Assoc., Inc.
1100 Glendon Ave. Suite 1200
Los Angeles, CA 90024

Heathkit
Heath Company
Benton Harbor, MI 49022

Karl Heitz
979 Third Ave.
New York, NY 10022

ISA (Information Security Assoc., Inc.)
65 Commerce Road
Stamford, CT 06904

ITI (Ion Track Instruments, Inc.)
109 Terrace Hall Ave.
Burlington, MA 01803

K-9 Command Dogs
3805 10th Ave.
New York, NY 10034

The Larder—Survival Books
11106 Magnolia Blvd.
North Hollywood, CA 91601

LEA (Law Enforcement Assoc.)
88 Holmes St.
Box 128
Belleville, NJ 07109

Mantis
P.O. Box 3749
Los Angeles, CA 90028

Markline
P.O. Box C-5
Belmont, MA 02178

Matthews Police Supply Co.
1441 West John St.
P.O. Box 1754
Matthews, NC 28105

Minolta Corporation
101 Williams Dr.
Ramsey, NJ 07446

Mountain West
4215 N. 16th St.
Box 10780
Phoenix, AZ 85064

On Guard Enterprises
P.O. Box 6341
Torrance, CA 90504

The Peterzell Co.
951 N. Pennsylvania Ave.
P.O. Box 966
Winter Park, FL 32790

Quality Creations
2801 Biscayne Dr.
Youngstown, OH 44505

Radio Shack
1300 One Tandy Center
Fort Worth, TX 76102

Rexell Shredders
5-17 48th Ave.
Long Island City, NY 11101

The Rouse School
    of Special Detective Training
P.O. Box 2469
Costa Mesa, CA 92626

Sears, Roebuck & Co.
Sears Tower
Chicago, IL 60684

Sharper Image
260 California St.
San Francisco, CA 94111

Streamlight Inc.
1030 West Germantown Pike
Norristown, PA 19403

Western States Sales and Marketing
3379 Cerritos Ave.
Los Alamitos, CA 90720